Wild Card

T0246226

The content of this book was carefully researched. All information is supplied without liability. Neither the authors nor the publisher will be liable for possible disadvantages, injuries, or damages.

Laura Siegemund
Prof. Dr. Stefan Brunner

Wild Card

Mastering the Mental Game
in Tennis, in Sport, and in Life

MEYER & MEYER SPORT

British Library of Cataloguing in Publication Data
A catalogue record is available from the British Library

Originally published as *Wild Card: Herausforderungen mental meistern*, © 2022 by Meyer & Meyer Verlag

Wild Card
Maidenhead: Meyer & Meyer Sport (UK) Ltd., 2024
ISBN: 978-1-78255-270-3

All rights reserved, especially the right to copy and distribute, including the translation rights. No part of this work may be reproduced–including by photocopy, microfilm or any other means–processed, stored electronically, copied or distributed in any form whatsoever without the written permission of the publisher.

© 2024 by Meyer & Meyer Sport (UK) Ltd.
Aachen, Auckland, Beirut, Cairo, Cape Town, Dubai, Hägendorf, Hong Kong, Indianapolis, Maidenhead, Manila, New Delhi, Singapore, Sydney, Tehran, Vienna

Member of the World Sport Publishers' Association, www.w-s-p-a.org

Printed by Versa Press, East Peoria, IL
Printed in the United States of America

ISBN: 978-1-78255-270-3
Email: info@m-m-sports.com
www.thesportspublisher.com

CONTENTS

Foreword by Dominik Klein **8**

Getting warmed up 10

**On the way to center court—the authors start
with an exchange of ideas** **10**

1 Starting the match 16

First serve: mastering the start **18**
Getting into the match 20
Teaching anxiety to be afraid 34
Creating one's own vibe 46
Preparing for the unexpected 57
Getting to know the opponent 65
Summary 71

2 The match picks up pace 72

Break and rebreak: being in the flow **74**
Understanding the match 75
The power of motivation 85
Goals propel us 101
A thousand hours of diligence 111
The enjoyment factor 116
Summary 127

3 Overcoming a point deficit 128

Lost set: turning crises into opportunities **130**
Overcoming adversity 133
Absorbing pressure 143
Processing errors and failure 152
Constructive mind games 163
Self-talk 171
Believing in yourself 177
Summary 183

4 Scoring the big points 184

Match point: being ready at the critical moment **186**
Once and never again 186
Maintaining routines and rituals 192
Summary 205

5 Personal development 206

Game, set, match: Designing careers **208**
Promising success 208
Searching for meaning and finding your identity 217
Handling mental and physical injuries 223
Safeguarding the quality of a career 240
Summary 252

Match analysis 255

**On the way to the locker room—
the authors' closing conversation** **255**

References 256
Index 264

FOREWORD

I have every reason to be grateful for my handball career. So much went according to plan: World Champion in 2007. That same year, I won the Champions League with THW Kiel—German Champion several times in a row. Yet in 2009, the break happened anyway: Heiner Brand did not nominate me for the 2010 European Championships. Ouch!

Getting psychological advice wasn't really a thing in men's handball. We're the toughest; we have no weaknesses. As a team, we go through thick and thin. But during this disappointing phase, I chose to see Jürgen Boss, a performance coach.

At the start of our first conversation, I was surprised when he repeatedly posed the same question: "What does it feel like when you're in good form? When you're on fire?" He wasn't satisfied with my answers until I nearly burst and jumped out of my seat and planted myself in front of him in typical handball defensive posture. My muscles were taut; my gaze was focused. "This is what it's like when I feel good!" He didn't have to ask again; I could suddenly feel it myself. That was it, precisely that feeling had been missing in recent months. The break was followed by a click.

After that I called him before every game. Sometimes we spoke for only three minutes. He asked simple questions and my answers tended to be the solution. Being able to find the solution yourself is the best way. We have to keep focusing on ourselves, take charge, make our own decisions. After all, it was *me* who decided to consult a coach, or to transfer to Nantes after ten years at the world-class club Kiel, or end my career at age thirty-four, even though I could have undoubtedly played longer.

And then there was a second break: in 2015, I tore my cruciate ligament. It was really my first injury. The day I was diagnosed was horrible. But one day after surgery, when I was still in my hospital bed, there was another click. I already had a plan, even a mantra: come back stronger!

I don't regret my injury. It provided a lot of clarity and propelled me forward. After eight months, I was back. Champions League group play. I subbed into the game for the final five minutes. We were one goal behind Veszprém. The first throw from a tight angle didn't go in.

But I didn't let that unnerve me. What helped was that I did lots of visualization during rehab. I mentally walked through lots of plays, even planned certain throwing scenarios. I even stood at the edge of my bed, rudimentarily simulated the throw, and let myself fall back onto the bed. My second throw was on target. Equalizer. And in the end, in almost the final second, I was able to score the winning goal. It was pure adrenaline and goosebumps!

The mental component in all of this is quite large. That's why it makes sense to create a repertoire in your head that you can tap into as needed. But sports psychology requires an athlete to be honest, otherwise it won't work. Rushing and giving instructions won't work. A better approach would be for a club or association to make the service available to everyone on a voluntary basis. Or you set an example or write a book or at least a preface.

And one more important thing: our basic attitude. When I talk about what makes a team successful, I always pose that question to the audience first. They have lots of suggestions, such as, for instance, passion, ambition, discipline. And those are all correct. But, to me, it is primarily something else. I believe it is mostly respect for each other. When eight different nationalities give it their all for a club, I feel deep gratitude and yes, respect.

—*Dominik Klein*
Hanball world champion, three-time winner of the Champions League, 187 games for the German national team

GETTING WARMED UP

ON THE WAY TO CENTER COURT— THE AUTHORS START WITH AN EXCHANGE OF IDEAS

Let's talk about success, Laura! Those who have it are happy, those who don't are sad. That seems like a blanket statement, but it's undeniably true. Success is how we measure and rank each other, and we unfortunately have no scruples secluding someone when they're unsuccessful. It is how we behave in sports, in society, in politics, and economics. We seek "formulas for success"; an internet search of the term will yield 1.5 million hits.

Absolutely, Stefan! Every ambitious person wants to leave no stone unturned. Everyone wants to be satisfied with himself and life and ideally—and that's an important point—receive recognition.

The high number of hits on the internet also proves that there isn't just one formula. The combination depends on the individual, on life context, and on the goals we set. This means the path to success can vary quite a bit.

That will be disappointing to many who would prefer a universal recipe for success. But it's not that simple. We are so different, even just in the way we think. The first important step toward success: we must realize that it's about finding our own path. And that depends on many aspects, as well as discipline and our attitude toward a challenge.

And talent of course plays a role. But as Malcolm Gladwell (2009) writes in his bestseller "Outliers: The Story of Success", performance does not primarily result from talent but from years of preparation. Only someone who has logged 10,000 practice hours can become a champion.

I agree with his sentiment. Success is largely based on diligence and hard work. No matter how great the talent, it alone will not produce success, and not in tennis either. A whole is made up of many individual pieces. I am not convinced by talent, but I do believe in diligence. I am certain that I achieved my own goals only through above-average discipline, endurance, and precisely-executed repetitions. That is a long-term process. We're not on YouTube where you can become famous and successful overnight.

Tennis is complex and offers many situations through which an athlete can and must grow if he wants to get to the top. It is a microcosm that can be easily applied to other competitive sports as well as life's overall challenges. In coaching, I often refer to analogies from tennis. For instance, the net cord shows how even small things can tip the balance. There's a fine line between luck and misfortune. The takeaway: we cannot control everything, no matter how much we want to.

That is my experience as well. In tennis I practice how to handle challenges I encounter in many other areas of my life. That is one of the reasons we chose to write this book together. I am convinced that our topics will resonate with every ambitious person. The problem-solving strategies that help me in tennis can be successfully applied to many other areas. Handling pressure, stress, and adversity—those are overarching challenges one must deal with at a certain level.

INTERVIEW

Gerd Schönfelder, ski racer and sixteen-time gold medalist in the Paralympics, once summarized it like this: "No matter how bad the initial situation, if you are mentally ready you can make it work for you." Our will is an important driver.

Tennis proves how much this driver can pay off. The scoring system alone provides every reason to want to hang on. Because as long as there is a theoretical chance, there is also hope. And as long as there is hope, we can believe in ourselves. Many seemingly hopeless matches have been turned around.

Let's take the 2022 tournament in Miami as an example: Five match points against you in the semi-final, all saved, and, in the end, winning the tournament. The ability to prevail in critical moments in tennis, as in life, pays off. There is lots of pressure to perform well, and thus also the necessity to process possible errors constructively.

Whether self-caused errors and missed chances in a match, or bitter losses or severe pain like, for instance, my torn anterior cruciate ligament (ACL) in 2017 at the height of my career, if you want to be successful, you have to learn to deal with mistakes and setbacks of all types. I also experienced that in the 2020 French Open. In spite of the miserable conditions, extremely cold temperatures, soaked courts, wind, and physical discomfort, I was able to achieve my best Grand Slam performance in singles. Success is no picnic; it requires a large amount of mental toughness.

. . . a very good example of less-than-perfect circumstances but a resounding success! Many expect to be perfect, and that becomes their undoing. Physical form alone varies from day to day, matches are rarely straightforward. What matters is to be mentally flexible, to self-optimize wisely instead of stoically perfecting. In tennis and in sports in general.

I tend to be a perfectionist. On the one hand, that is what drove me and brought me very far. On the other hand, I was often my own worst enemy due to excessive ambition and perfectionism. That caused me to not appreciate my developmental process separate from the results. Only when I allowed myself to be more relaxed was I able to really achieve my potential.

Particularly in elite sports, letting go sometimes can be very difficult. A change of perspective is often helpful. We remove ourselves from our personal experiences and instead look at ourselves from the outside, from the view of the coach, the fans, a good friend, or the opponent. We are familiar with this process from systemic therapy.

This outside perspective really helped me. Even as an experienced player, I frequently fall back into the old thought-and-behavior patterns. In those moments, when I make life difficult for myself, a conscious change of perspective helps me.

And that skill cannot be trained. The psyche must be trained and many don't realize that. After 2007, when the top athlete Magdalena Neuner began working with a mental coach, she claimed that people shook their heads in disbelief. Mental training is part of the preparation for competing at the world-class level from the start, meaning it is part of the previously mentioned 10,000-hours rule.

Ten thousand hours is a long time to keep up motivation. That requires a fire that feeds everything, and that can never go out. There was a time when I could no longer feel that fire. I had to think about on my course and correct it. During the Covid-19 pandemic, some players openly talked about having lost their inner fire and decided to end their career.

INTERVIEW

Keeping up one's ambition for years and decades really is a major task. Interruptions in physical form and motivation will happen. And that flame can also get smaller. He exists, the star who stands on the stage in front of thousands of spectators and afterwards is oblivious to his good fortune, is unable to feel euphoric, not even satisfied, in spite of his success. Golf legend Bernhard Langer once told me how, after winning his first major tournament and becoming number one in the world rankings, he lay in bed on Sunday night after the celebration and only felt emptiness. You have to learn to cope with such a situation and feeling.

External success isn't automatically internal success and satisfaction. Precisely that is the reason why it is important to shift the focus to one's personal development process while still keeping our eye on the goal. With all that laser focus on the top, we can't forget to put one foot in front of the other and must have the courage and permit ourselves to occasionally take a turn and enjoy the view.

Bringing together all of the experiences in this book, and using that information to develop impulses that help us handle challenging tasks, will be an exciting journey.

That is why the title of our book is *Wild Card*. It stands for getting an opportunity to achieve something awesome and surprising yourself and others. Like me in 2017, when I was able to win the Porsche Tennis Grand Prix in Stuttgart with a wild card, one of the greatest singles successes of my career. A wild card also represents something we don't know yet and that doesn't always follow the usual rules. But at the same time, the card also means responsibility for the one who receives it and whose potential has been recognized.

We hope that our readers will recognize their personal wild card in this book and thus take the opportunity and benefit from our symbiosis: combining our vast worlds of experience in sports, coaching and science.

INTERVIEW

1
Starting
the match

© dpa picture alliance

FIRST SERVE: MASTERING THE START

Erich Kästner, an expert par excellence in sports psychology! Yes? One would expect many different names in this first chapter. But the fact that Erich Kästner takes the very first spot in a mental reference book might raise some eyebrows. At least at first. The creator of *Pünktchen und Anton* advising psychologists and others?

Absolutely, because Kästner proved to have very good instincts for the peculiarities of sports in general: "Skiers fight the clock. Swimmers compete side-by-side. Pole vaulters compete one after the other." And tennis players in particular: "It is uncertain who will become the winner until the final minute."[1] Kästner thereby stated a peculiarity of the sport of tennis that is fundamental to the psyche: The rules do not set a time limit. Whoever scores the last point, wins. Players are therefore able to believe in themselves until the very end, even if the current score suggests otherwise.

But how can we sustain that faith in ourselves, develop it, or even just inspire it?

Nowadays, sports psychology draws on decades of experience. Scientific findings combined with the huge amount of experience of elite athletes and other performance-oriented people show promising strategies, as discussed in this book. But no matter how quick and explosive the athlete might normally get off the starting block, it takes some time for the athlete to recognize the power of mental influence.

Here Erich Kästner was quicker. His insights came way back in the last century, which posthumously makes him one of the originators of sports psychology.

It was the 1980s, when the legendary ski racer Frank Wörndl also began mental training. He sought advice from the sports psychologist Hans Eberspächer, became World Champion in 1987, and took second place in the 1988 Olympics. Wörndl attributed his success in part to

---

1   Kästner (n. d.).

their collaboration.[2] His insight was foresight and also uncommon for some time to come.

Team athletes in particular took longer to recognize the expanded opportunities via psychological training. Soccer players in particular struggled. Back in 1998, at the World Cup in France, hardly any national teams sought mental support.[3] A soccer player seeking psychological support? He or she would have been viewed as a weak patient rather than a highly professional athlete who simply buckles down and gives it their all.

Mental work was uncommon for a long time, agrees the exceptional biathlete, Magdalena Neuner. When she started to work with a mental coach in 2007, "everyone sneered at me." But she thought it was important to realize and tap her full potential. Psychology to gain an edge on the others? "I wanted to try it. We worked with the subconscious and I learned a lot about myself."

The necessity of psychological interventions

When asking a sports-minded crowd, everyone can name a whole list of classic coaches, but hardly anyone knows a sports psychologist. They work in the background, even though their work is very important. Even the media has little interest in this occupational group. Next to head coaches, the most popular interviewees are former athletes and maybe tactical experts. Physiologists, nutritionists, athletic trainers, and sports psychology coaches exist in the periphery of the training staff and are therefore easily overlooked.

Maybe we need a few Erich Kästners who can cast more of a spotlight on all relevant areas of training. After all, in his statements he already emphasized focus, intuition, humor, composure, self-control, and reason as important qualities in an athlete.[4]

---

2   Brunner (1998).
3   Ibidem.
4   Kästner (n. d.).

Meanwhile elite sports have gotten very competitive. One time Mikaela Shiffrin wins, the next time it's Vlhová. One time it's Rafael Nadal, then it's Novak Djokovic. One time it's Real Madrid and then Bayern Munich. One-hundredth of a second is enough and a lucky goal during stoppage time is, too. The athletes are well-trained physically. But there is a growing realization that a coach alone is unable to address all of the partial aspects that need to be developed.

This set off the starting gun—by now heard by everyone—for a care team that is broad in scope and in which sports psychology has an important place. However, top-golfer Bernhard Langer contends: "Anyone who claims that 90 percent of golf is mental is wrong."[5] But he is convinced that "when two players are equally good, the mentally stronger one will win."

GETTING INTO THE MATCH

When at the 2014 soccer World Championships, Brazil lost against Germany 1–7, it took only six minutes to score four goals. An historic World Cup record; a negative record for Brazil. A top athlete's attention span just won't tolerate a momentary lapse, not in soccer, not in tennis, and not in many other sports.

The initial phase of a competition is particularly precarious. The working temperature must be spot on, muscle tone must be right, body and mind must be attuned to the competition. "Sleeping" through the start, missing the first few minutes—that could be the beginning of a loss. Winning that special opening game at a soccer World Cup after a point deficit is statistically nearly impossible. So far, it has only happened twice: Chile in 1962 and Brazil in 2014.

That means it's important to function immediately, beginning with the first serve. But how does one do that, in sports and in general? We all know the admonishment of having missed the start and therefore having fallen behind. It has given rise to many well-known sayings, such as *having your back to the wall* or to *have blown it*. There is a lot of room

---

5   Brunner (2020, pg. 48).

for improvement, and that has to be used. Meeting one's full potential from the first second on is important.

A good start is essential at world-class level. To be all in starting with the very first point, to immediately seize those first opportunities and—even more importantly—to send a message to the opponent from the get-go: Today will be difficult for you! You will be punished for all your mistakes!

The start of a match, those initial points are also extremely important. Sure, I'll get second chances over the course of the game. And the counting system in tennis will theoretically give me a chance until the end to turn the game around. But the higher the playing level, and the more resolute and consistent the opponents, the smaller are my theoretical chances for correcting my own mistakes.

That means I need a good start, I need to quickly implement my planned strategy, and quickly reach my performance limit on that day.

I have to start right at the starting whistle. Performance initially increases in direct proportion to increasing activation. If activation is too high, the performance curve can actually flatten again. Consequently, the goal is to find the individually appropriate activation potential and store it in body and mind where it can be retrieved.

Yuri L. Hanin, long-time professor at the Research Institute for Olympic Sports in Finland, quite appropriately calls it the "individual zones of optimal functioning."[6] The model makes it possible to identify a current "biopsychosocial state." This emotional parameter is closely linked to additional requirements for a human being's general functioning, linked, for instance, to the general, subjective sense of well-being as well as competition-related emotions.

---

6   Hanin (2000).

A speaker on a stage must captivate the audience with his first impression. He can be surprising, convincing, and depending on the type, can even be provocative, funny, shocking, or offer solidarity. The possibilities are abundant. The choice depends on many independent variables, especially the situation and the audience. When applied to real-life situations, this means: The speaker who intends to spend an evening with his audience must meet his counterparts, must unite with them. Rhetoric experts advise that he must love his audience.

The athlete who wishes to quickly neutralize his opponent of course follows a different strategy. But what both situations have in common is that the initial moments are important and potentially decisive.

Getting into the optimal pre-start state isn't easy. Sure, over time an athlete develops routines that help him prepare for a task. Ideally, with more experience, the process will become faster and better and can ultimately be applied to different situations. What matters is: there is no right or wrong! Everyone has to find out for him/herself what his optimal activation level feels like and how they can achieve it. Recapping how one has prepared on a day with a particularly good performance can be helpful here.

- *What did it feel like?*
- *What worked particularly well to clear my head during preparation?*
- *Also: what was counterproductive and should definitely not be repeated during preparation?*

I have tried many things: For example, listening to hard rock during the final minutes before a match to really put myself in the zone. In recent years, I have increasingly based my preparation on how I am feeling at that moment. Personally, for an optimal performance, my personal activation level must be pretty high from the start.

> *I don't have a textbook approach that I go to every time, but rather an arsenal of tools I choose from depending on my mental and physical state. What matters to me is being able to withdraw to a quiet place. A separate room is usually best. There I am also able to build in a brief meditation if I notice that, although necessary, I am just too keyed up.*

At the start, activation can be too high but also too low. One can come to a job interview, a meeting, or presentation overly nervous or slightly lethargic. No matter where and when the situation occurs, we must have the appropriate amount of activation to complete the task.

This insight goes back more than 100 years. The American psychologists Robert Yerkes and John Dodson were already testing on rats at the start of the last century what later was transferred to humans: an inverted u-shaped relationship between arousal and performance with respect to learning tasks. It turns out that the best performance implementation occurs at a medium arousal level. In psychology this scientific finding is referred to as the **Yerkes-Dodson law.**[7]

When someone gets overexcited—like the stereo that is turned up so loud that it can only produce a distorted cacophony—they are tensed up in the physical and literal sense. From a sports perspective, competition excitement comes face-to-face with competition apathy.[8] Mental tension benefits performance until it reaches a certain level, at which point, the benefits taper off again.

For instance, the runner describes it as getting "tight." When looking at heart rate, the optimal pulse range of a twenty-year-old during a tennis serve lies between 120 and160 beats per minute.[9] These numbers alone show that being aware of the optimal activation level isn't easy: it's a wide range, the difference between 120 and 160 heartbeats is significant, regardless of age.

---

7   Yerkes & Dodson (1908).
8   Puni (1961).
9   Burchard (2015).

And we're then supposed to find our place in this generous range. It's difficult! It depends on the individual. It depends on the fitness level. And it depends on the challenge. When applied to sports, it means that the 100-meter sprinter requires a different level of activation to the marathon runner, the boxer, the platform diver, or sport shooter.

It's similar to the different situations of major challenges in other areas of life. Pilots and teachers, rock musicians, and radio hosts—they all perform at varying levels of excitement due to their professional challenges.

Regulating tonus up or down—more on that in a minute—is relatively easy. However, finding one's own best tone is a process that requires experience, patience, and sensitivity. One thing is for certain, the right heart beat cannot be looked up in a textbook. We must feel our most effective tonus. W. Timothy Gallwey calls it "relaxed concentration."[10]

At first glance, an oxymoron; at second glance, an interesting idea because it offers a path to body awareness: making it perceptible by noticing the differences between varying degrees of muscular tension.

Tonus as an important indicator

Progressive muscle relaxation, PMR for short, was developed in 1929 by the American physiologist Edmund Jacobson,[11] and is a scientifically proven method that allows us this view inside the body. Muscles and muscle groups are successively tightened and relaxed so we can experience the possible tonus as a kind of continuum. The challenge is finding the right setting on this continuum for a particular situation. What is the right amount for me?

---

10   Gallwey (2015).
11   Jacobson (2011).

This frequently used question is helpful here:

- When did it feel good?

- Did my perceived state of tension benefit the situation?

- When were my focus, my concentration, my awareness and atten-tiveness, my **flow**, best when the referee blew the starting whistle?

That is how I am able to overlay the feel of external practice incremen-tally with the feel of my actual playing until the two perfectly overlap.

Like a piano tuner whose perfect ear can ascertain the smallest acous-tic vibrations and eliminate any tonal imbalances. But PMR-originator Jacobson looked at muscular imbalances. He recognized the directly proportional relationship between muscle tension and excitement.

In medical terms, activity triggers the sympathetic nervous system, which then triggers muscle tension. It is fortunate, but also nature's sensible protective mechanism that we don't have to tolerate unlimited amounts of this escalation. As previously mentioned, we are able to lower the tonus and thereby bring the opposite of the sympathetic nervous system—the parasympathetic nervous system—into the game to save us.

There are multiple ways to do so, all of which are considered relaxation methods: the previously mentioned PMR, **breathing exercises** and auto-suggestion methods such as **autogenic training** and guided imagery.

Sport shooter Barbara Engleder struggled for years with the physical effects of a pulse that was too high and raised the front of her weapon, in time with her pulse. With ingenious timing, she was able to pull the trigger whenever her pulse allowed. The effective method: "Progressive muscle relaxation helped me. And I worked a lot with breathing exercises."

There is scientific evidence that not only the muscles relax, but PMR also calms blood pressure, heart rate, breathing, and intestinal activity.[12] Furthermore, this exercise is so easy to implement—even while sitting down—that it has already proven effective during childhood and adolescence and can lead to independent practice.[13] Autogenic training tends to appeal more to adults. The more vivid guided imagery variation was developed for children.

The power of autosuggestion

Both techniques create a sense of heaviness and warmth, among other things, that facilitates relaxation and helps lower the tonus. Autogenic training is also based on scientific findings.

Easier yet: Breathing techniques are an independent relaxation method, but they are also used in preparation for other methods. As inhalation is automatic, the focus here is primarily on exhalation during which the ribcage relaxes. Even just focusing on exhalation leads to a sense of relaxation.[14]

The scientists Anne-Marie Elbe and Jürgen Beckmann point to an additional advantage of breathing exercises: While techniques such as autogenic training generally lower the overall activation level, breathing relaxation interferes less with the competition tonus. It can also simply help us focus on the impending activity or breathe away disruptive thoughts.

---

12   Gröninger & Stade-Gröninger (1996).
13   Brunner (2002).
14   Beckmann & Elbe (2008, pg. 53).

If I want to regain my focus and generally be able to see clearly, I try to find my inner calm. For me the quickest way to do so is with brief breathing exercises during the change of ends. I put those 90 seconds to use, close my eyes, try to shift my focus inward, and leave everything else outside.

The music intended to create a party atmosphere in the stands during the change of ends, the spectators' celebration, the score announcements coming from the adjacent courts. Everything slowly fades from my consciousness. I am focused completely inward, inhale and exhale deeply, feel my Qi[15] flow through my body like a wave.

When I have trouble shifting my focus inward, I focus it on a particular area of my body, for instance how my feet touch the ground or my bottom and my back nestling against my seat. I think about nothing and just take a brief break from everything.

I don't worry about the score, about the next service, about the consequences of my performance. For a few seconds, I simply exist and focus on my breath.

When the referee calls "time" I open my eyes and make a tactical plan for the impending game on my way to the baseline. I feel refreshed, my head feels lighter as though I left baggage behind on the bench. I am now able to focus on my task.

So, we can assign specific tasks to our inhalation and exhalation: As I inhale, I breathe in fresh energy; as I exhale, I let go of old unnecessary burdens such as, for instance, intrusive thoughts.

---

15 Vital energy.

"It was incredibly helpful", says Michael Niedermeier, two-time artistic cycling World Champion. "The breathing techniques allowed me to better manage my nerves,"[16] explained judoka Theresa Stoll. In 2021, she won mixed-team bronze at the Tokyo Olympics.

Some helpful relaxation tools stem from that region. Far Eastern techniques like Qigong, Tai-Chi, and yoga also have a tonus-regulating effect. And sometimes we are able to relax by simply having a conversation that helps us organize the confusion in our heads and reveals a guiding thread.

2016 marked the first time I made it to the second round of the Australian Open and also the first time I played in a really big stadium, back then at the Hisense Arena against Jelena Janković, as the number 19 seed. I was extremely nervous before the match and absolutely did not want to play below my potential. I was in good spirits and sensed that I had a realistic chance of winning.

I was extremely tense. My usual routines were supposed to fix it and help me calm down: warming up with my coach, taking time between practice and the match—to change and fastidiously prepare my gear—my usual warm-up exercises right before the match to raise my temperature.

But none of those things helped that day. Shortly before the match, right during my warm-up, I talked to my coach. I explained that I felt much too tense and asked to see him for a few minutes in private; a conversation in a quiet corner somewhere in the catacombs of the Rod Laver Arena, far from all the other players who were at that moment sprinting through the hallways, were tossing balls back and forth with their fitness coaches, or pulling on resistance bands.

---

16   Brunner (2017a).

I knew I needed that before entering the stadium. That verbalizing once more where we stood at this point in my career, what we intended to do during this important match, and how we would implement it, would help me. So, on the one hand, we talked about the tactical and playing goals of this particular match, but on the other hand, also about the significance in a larger context.

After that conversation my head was clearer, I was calmer, everything was sorted. I knew—and that was very important—where I stood and where we wanted to go. I could see the map. Now I just had to go out and follow it.

Sometimes a strategic use of time helps, like a brief conversation just before the match or during the break, to reset the mind. Playing can also help over time by disrupting the opponent's rhythm and finding your own rhythm again.

Buying time means securing valuable moments for physical and mental regeneration, like the tennis player who changes rackets. But situations from very different areas of life can also be good examples. Someone participating in a meeting or an assembly can typically excuse themselves to use the restroom to clear their head and gather their thoughts.

We don't always have to bring rhythm to chaos; we don't always tend to excessive activation. Sometimes a lack of motivation can bring us to our knees. It can extend all the way to permanent fatigue, which can be part of a depressive episode as defined in the ICD 10, the World Health Organization's (WHO) international classification of diseases.[17]

Sensitivity to the despondency of many people is absolutely essential. According to a survey from 2021, 4.2 percent of people in Germany alone suffer from **burnout**.[18]

---

17   Federal Institute for pharmaceuticals and medical devices (2019).
18   Statista Research Department (2012).

That means every twenty-fifth person suffers from this type of exhaustion. And it can be assumed that there are many more that were not captured (more on that in chapter 5).

Let us stay with the harmless variation of a lack of motivation, a tonus that is temporarily below threshold. Situations always require spontaneous and fast energizing, particularly at the moment of the start: the 100-meter runner and the 100-meter swimmer before the starting signal, the ball-sport athletes before the starting whistle, the sledders when they enter the ice tunnel.

Psyching up can be easily observed in boxers and alpine ski racers who pound their chests immediately before they start, regardless of gender. Olympic champion in skeleton Hannah Neise slapped her thighs before her successful individual slides. It is a tactile wake-up call intended to generate a high level of pre-start activation in the body. It is also an archaic symbol of strength.

A good example from the somewhat less complex animal world is the male gorilla. This kind of behavior is unfortunately not appropriate in the public outside of sports. Otherwise, the manager would do well to pound his chest to draw strength before a presentation. Alas, he would be better off doing so in the privacy of his office or the restroom.

The gesture is often accompanied by acoustics to emphasize this type of soliloquy: "Come on!" became the motivational slogan across the world. But commanding oneself to perform can also be done silently and inward. Instead of shouting, thoughts can be just as effective. And the manager would not have to go to another room.

Quick movements like, for instance, the bob and weave of tennis players or the brief sprints of soccer players prior to the starting whistle, also facilitate **activation**. Deliberately increasing the respiratory rate is also activating. The authors Beckman and Elbe add activating images to the list[19] and use the example of a 400-meter runner who imagined herself running the track with the momentum of a cougar.

---

19   Beckman & Elbe (2008, pg. 66).

The idea of this visualized activation can be applied to all areas of life. Like the example of the cougar, the animal world provides suitable visual inspiration, especially when it comes to movement. The mental movie screen can show a cheetah pursuing his prey.

The plant world can also provide suitable inspiration, particularly when it comes to stability. For instance, a tree can provide suitable metaphors about fortitude to the brain. Imagining cheering crowds of people can most likely also counter the sadness that was felt by many athletes when stadiums had to close their gates due to Covid-19.

It was anything but easy during the coronavirus pandemic, playing without spectators, in front of empty stands. Missing was the "hype" that has a major effect on the subjective feeling about an impeding task. There were no interviews before a game or even a tournament. Even the big entrance show fell victim to Covid.

On the court, I often felt a lack of tension, and my activation level wasn't on par with the importance of the task. To increase activation to the appropriate level, we had to actively tell ourselves the importance of a point or a game.

While I did achieve my best Grand Slam result overall at the French Open in October 2020, getting there was a rocky road. My body and my mind struggled with the miserable weather conditions and empty stands. Without the energy of the spectators, the fantastic atmosphere at a Grand Slam tournament, and the accompanying tension, it was hard to stay focused. Everything felt lax, unmotivated.

> *In many situations I didn't have the necessary tension needed to play my best. It didn't matter whether it was the best rally of my life or a serious mistake, either way there was no spectator response. The court remained dead silent.*
>
> *When I was far behind during the first set of one of my first matches, my perceived activation level was at zero. I chose an unusual strategy. Ordinarily, before the big points, I would never want to think about how many points on the ranking list, how much money and prestige were at stake with the next point.*
>
> *But that is precisely what I needed at that moment without tension and elevated pulse: feeling the importance of the next point in my body and my head. Building the necessary tension when it didn't happen on its own.*
>
> *I did some quick sprints and tapping in place, purposefully accelerating and regulating my breathing, and tried to thereby increase my heart rate. At the same time, I thought about how important that next point was, the significance of a loss or win to my career.*
>
> *Sure, it was peculiar and the opposite of what I would do in a similar situation under normal circumstances. But at that moment it was my salvation, and it worked.*

And then there is the power of **music**. For instance, when looking around the stadium during the Olympics, one can see many athletes lying down, sitting, walking, with eyes open and closed, with a towel over their head or around their shoulders, and, well, music on their ears. Some athletes may bring in their influencer ambitions, feel obligated to get their headphone brand on camera. But they, like all the others inside the stadium, use the effects of music.

Evidence of how music affects our emotions can be traced all the way back to antiquity.[20] Research on the effects of bass and beat has been going on for a long time and concluded that "music with a strong experience maxim within a piece and a slow but powerful climax at the end, will be experienced as very exciting,"[21] according Herbert Bruhn and a team of authors. Furthermore "pleasurable movement sensations" can be triggered in the brain when listening to music louder than ninety decibels. Here, the researchers refer to Neil McAngus Todd, who boldly talks about the "rock 'n' roll threshold." The trigger is said to be the sacculus, part of the head's vestibular system, which otherwise is responsible for maintaining balance.

Music can help the mind organize itself and thus "reduces mental entropy or the subordination we experience when random information interferes with our goals,"[22] says happiness researcher Mihaly Csikszentmihalyi. "Music can trigger flow."

So, using music to make certain moments memorable or letting waves of music trigger certain emotions is far more than sentimentalism.

The world-famous German jazz musician Klaus Doldinger knows this. He likes it when participants of a jam session play with vigor. "When the musicians I play with bring it, I get swept up. It gets me going."[23]

People get teary-eyed at the opera and feel captivated by the overture the orchestra is playing, fans at the soccer stadium belt out their club's hymn with emotion, the national anthem lends solemnity to an honor ceremony. Cinematic use of a heartbeat put to the images creates drama; the images become secondary.

---

20   Bruhn et al. (2008, pg. 548).
21   Ibidem, pg. 526, as cited in McAngus Todd (2000).
22   Csikszentmihalyi (2017) pg. 175).
23   Brunner (2017b, pg. 83).

In an interview with the newspaper *Süddeutsche Zeitung*, Ron-Thorben Hoffman, contract goalkeeper at Bayern Munich on loan to AFC Sunderland in England, described the goosebumps moment: "Before the starting whistle, when the fans sing the Elvis classic 'Can't help falling in love.' Afterwards they yell 'Sunderland!', so loud that the entire stadium shakes for a moment."[24]

Beckmann and Elbe point out one more important scientific finding, that performance depends less on physical excitement and more on the athlete's **individual assessment of the situation**. This also applies to the classification of one's own competition-related tension. If it is classified as too high and talked up as unwanted nervousness, it can inhibit confident action orientation.[25]

But if that same tension is interpreted as a necessary reaction to a challenge, it can result in motivation and focused action. One thing is for sure, after all these statements, we cannot fail to recognize what sport shooter and gold medal winner Barbara Engleder describes as the pleasant first impression: "That first shot can generate an important feeling. If it was good, it is much easier for me to get into the competition."

TEACHING ANXIETY TO BE AFRAID

A completely undesirable feeling before a start is **anxiety**, something that is expressed with a variety of words and absolutely must be differentiated. **Nervousness, shyness, agitation,** and **stage fright** are examples of terms used to describe fear. Differentiation isn't always easy. For instance, the transition from stage fright to performance anxiety, from a musician's point of view, is "fluid."[26]

No matter how we label that feeling, what matters is at what point it inhibits our ability to fulfill tasks. Consequently, this raises the question of if and possibly when and how often we get to that point. Recognizing this critical point is also vital.

---

24 Hopper (2021, pg. 26).
25 Beckmann & Elbe (2008, pg. 56f.)
26 Mumm et al. (2020, pg. 75).

We know from everyday life that limits cannot simply be moved back and forth. Limits—and this we also know from everyday life—can also be avoided or sometimes evaded.

This is where it gets interesting. We are able to determine our options for avoiding unwanted emotional states, although here sports are different from most other areas: they are competitive by nature. A play or musical performance, which also depends on public performance, are generally not competitive.

But let's take a look at musicians. How do they handle **performance anxiety**? An unsteady finger on the fingerboard of a violin is as disastrous as a shaky note when singing. Trembling as the physical manifestation of inner imbalance must also be avoided at all cost.

"Acting is a scary profession," said the famous stage performer Nicholas Ofczarek in January 2022 in an interview. "Anxiety and shame were my constant companions during rehearsals."[27]

And this member of the Vienna Burgtheater describes another, often unseen aspect of anxiety: concomitant fatigue. "Being constantly overwhelmed by anxiety is exhausting." Getting rid of anxiety or at least mitigating it and learning to manage it is a worthwhile but, of course, not entirely easy endeavor—considering that some subliminal pre-start anxiety can also have an attention-activating benefit.

Systematic desensitization is one form of anxiety control during which the affected person confronts himself with anxiety situations, mentally or visually with photos and videos, in hierarchical order. Starting with the weakest anxiety-inducing trigger, the subject tries to make himself more resilient in specific situations, step-by-step. The technical term is raising **resilience**.

---

27   Michaelsen (2022).

Relaxation techniques as a proven method

And how does the Burgtheater actor pull himself out of this misery? "I tell myself as often as possible, "Niki, you know it's ok to start at zero every time!" In the past he also used **relaxation exercises**. It is a good intuitive choice, its effectiveness confirmed by the team of authors working with psychologist Jennifer Mumm who has been doing research at the Berlin Center for Musicians' Medicine at the Charité since 2018.

Relaxation helps to manage anxiety, increases general well-being, and provides a balance to stress.[28]

The Austrian Ofczarek adds another highly interesting aspect: "The strange thing is that I get really calm when the auditorium fills up during the final rehearsals. I feel protected by the audience and the anxiety is suddenly gone." Be honest! Who would think of turning the group of people that causes uncertainty and anxiety into the opposite, a thera-peutic team that offers safety and security?!

Of course, not everything that causes worry can be turned into a good luck charm at the drop of a hat. But this depiction of an impressive pivot should not be reduced to a day-and-night change.

The more obvious and less curious conception would be a gentle shift on a continuum. This is very much in line with the Israeli-American me-dical sociologist Aaron Antonovsky's findings, who in the 1970s coined the term **salutogenesis**, referring to the fluid transition from illness to health.[29] Meaning, he did not believe that the two seemingly opposing terms were a dichotomy. One is not exclusively one thing or another, but rather parts of both.

Here the transfer to stage fright and pre-start anxiety, on the one hand, and to self-assuredness and self-confidence, on the other hand, pro-vides opportunities. The proverbial black-and-white thinking has long

---

28   Mumm et al. (2020).
29   Antonovsky (1997).

been disqualified as a generalizing and thus unsuitable category system. But now as before, it still creeps into our consciousness as an annoying evaluation scheme. Antonovsky's suggestion should give us sufficient reason to ignore it and take differentiating measures.

Anxiety has the awful desire to spread and overshadow everything else. Starting now, we will resist because we are aware that our similarly inclined self-confidence doesn't disappear only because anxiety wants to extinguish it. Thus, we practice viewing our emotions on a continuum and judiciously sliding the regulator bit by bit in the desired direction.

The famous German singer Helene Fischer most likely did the same. Earlier in her career, an impending performance made her very nervous. But over the years, it turned into "pure anticipation." That is what she told interviewer Sven Gätjen in November 2021, in a *Sat.1* interview and added, that the basic tension she feels before a performance is also "incredibly stimulating."

Here, too, one might ask how nervousness can simply be transformed into anticipation. That idea is inherent in the same, previously mentioned, impulse to view oneself on a continuum.

- What does anxiety even mean?

- When does it become a problem and when does it become pathologic?

Anxiety is cause for concern when it occurs in "objectively non-dangerous situations, when we are unable to control it, and it leads to performance losses and subjective suffering."[30] Or when the condition is "characterized by tormenting, lasting anxiety or inappropriate behaviors to relieve anxiety."[31]

---

30 Mumm et al. (2020, pg. 75)
31 Myers (2008, pg. 756).

Learning to understand anxiety

Anxiety can sometimes be traced back to evolutionary biology, and some people can have a "genetic predisposition to be anxious about certain things and develop anxiety more so than others."[32] Only the repeated occurrence of anxiety episodes can be evidence of a permanent disorder.

For instance, phobias, panic attacks, obsessive-compulsive disorder (OCD), and post-traumatic stress disorder (PTSD) are abnormal anxiety manifestations and will not be discussed further. But one episode, the **panic attack**, must still be taken seriously. It can "be an important indicator of possible stress overload."[33]

Adaptive disorders are also common. They can be triggered by, for instance, a change in workplace or training location.

In a sports context we differentiate between **state anxiety** and **trait anxiety**. State anxiety is caused by a situation that feels threatening, such as when a game against a fierce opponent is imminent. Or when we have to compete in an unfamiliar location. Or when we are inhibited by fear of injury. Or when we are afraid of embarrassing ourselves because we lack confidence in the task.

We feel overwhelmed and are uncertain. Formidable opponents, fear of injury, fear of embarrassment, failure, a blow to one's image, social decline—the overwhelming power of the feeling is crushing.

---

32   Ibidem, (pg. 763).
33   Staufenbiel et al. (2019).

State anxiety has a cognitive component—apprehension—and a somatic component that reflects one's perception of the own anxiety and manifests itself in muscle tension and increased heart rate.[34] The permanent performance-related situations in sports lead to many such moments. But we ultimately encounter performance-related situations in all areas of life where an expectation is placed on us.

The type of anxiety that can be a permanent part of someone's personality but can also provoke state anxiety is different because someone who is anxious also feels threatened more quickly. In this case, it should be clear that learning more about an athlete's disposition is essential as well as beneficial.

Performance diagnosis via questionnaire

There are standard questionnaires for both types of anxiety—state and trait—to get a sense of the athlete's personality and help create a basis for performance diagnosis.

There is broad consensus that anxiety is not a good counselor when it comes to exploiting one's performance capacity because "there is a lack of ease and motor coordination suffers; decisions are often not situation-appropriate; adaptation to the next task is not optimal; and learning is impaired."[35]

When anxiety becomes a constantly recurring feeling, another variant typically emerges that one absolutely wants to avoid: **fear of anxiety**, fear of fear. It not only appears sooner than the actual anxiety but also paves the way for anxiety as a kind of self-fulfilling prophecy.

---

34   Güllich & Krüger (2013, pg. 296).
35   Beckmann & Elbe (2008, pg. 119).

Before my matches, I was and am typically extremely nervous. Nervousness and anxiety live very close together, the transitions are fluid. Anxiety and doubt were always my steady companions. And that's nothing to be ashamed of. To the contrary. I think most high performers have fears and doubts, not least of all because they are perfectionists and believe that only the best will do. Some just hide it better than others.

To up my game, it was very important that I learned how to better manage these feelings. In tennis one can be afraid of playing poorly and can doubt the ability to tap one's full potential and therefore lose. During a match, fears can emerge, hard-earned opportunities can be left unexploited, seeing everything on a silver tray in front of you and still failing, for instance while leading 5:2 in the third set of an important match.

It is not unusual to feel an impending humiliation during a phase in the game in which one hasn't even made many mistakes. Anxiety, fear, and doubt start in the head, but quickly affect the body. They cause excessive activation, make us jittery. Then it is difficult to calm down and keep a clear head.

Worst-case scenario, anxiety can be paralyzing so that we lose access to our body. What's really bad is when we already anticipate anxiety and failure and they actually occur as the result of a self-fulfilling prophecy.

"The issue of nausea, it's the first time I'm talking about it"—that was the title of the *Spiegel* interview with soccer pro Per Mertesacker on March 9, 2018.[36] Before games he apparently also experienced tremors so severe in his left foot that they made his comforter rustle. Mertesacker talked about pressure and the fear of "always looking at the scoreboard and counting the minutes. But at the World Cup, that was cruel."

---

36   Windmann (2018).

His is not an isolated case, but it is not talked about, especially not in the soccer community. This concealing and hiding has negative consequences. In 2009, the goalkeeper Robert Enke died. He concealed his depression. Fear became his undoing in two ways: fears that caused him to become depressed and the fear of going public.

It is a vicious cycle, and there are many vicious cycles within this context. The "vicious cycle of fear" used by the therapist for transparency can also be applied to sports. But we will start by calling it the slightly milder "vicious cycle of uncertainty."

A possible scenario: the soccer player who is subbed in late in the game as a super sub is already nervous and now has to prove his ability in a short period of time. The first two touches go badly. Instead of playing the first ball to his teammate, he plays it to the feet of the opponent; the second pass goes out of bounds. The sub begins to doubt himself. At the same time, he assumes that his weak entrance wasn't lost on the spectators. And definitely not on the coach. "Does he regret having subbed me in?"

These thoughts distract from the game, he loses his focus, and his mental state goes downhill. His physical state also takes a hit; movements become erratic. Precise and deliberate passing is hardly possible. The anxiety reaches the next level, and the vicious cycle tightens the next noose around its victim.

The sooner one can break out of this vicious cycle the easier it is. It would have been best if the soccer player in the above example had been able to break up those automated thoughts right after the second bad pass. To not put himself in the spectators' and coach's shoes— those mind games would only be speculative and in no way reliable— and come to the realization that two of two touches have no statistical bearing on his game.

We should practice putting things in perspective and reframing them as often as possible. Psychologists Beckmann and Elbe recommend analyzing the risk potential and then assigning it the name "fear," because we understand this name as "an emotional response to concrete, easily identifiable stimuli that signal danger." Consequently, fear can be channeled into specific avoidance responses that correspond to the fear-inducing stimuli, which can thereby be diminished.[37] Reframing anxiety and countering it with a different attitude is a tried and tested method that helps many athletes.

Even if it feels incredibly unpleasant in the hours and minutes before a match, I know that a pretty high tension level and nervousness are necessary for my performance.

During my career, three steps have helped me cope with nervousness as well as with anxiety and doubt.

- *First step: Understanding where those feelings are coming from.*
- *Second step: Accepting those feelings.*
- *Third step: Consciously countering those feelings.*

About "understanding": It helped me to understand much better where those fears and doubts were coming from, the real reason.

- *What is causing the fear of losing this final?*
- *Is it the match itself?*
- *Is it the specific opponent?*
- *Or is it the fear of missing an opportunity to win a tournament?*

Fear is often caused by the enormous feeling of singularity, the feeling of having only one chance, and that this chance may never come again.

---

37   Beckmann & Elbe (2008, pg. 119).

When fear and doubt get to be too much, I talk to a trusted person, for example, my coach or my sports psychologist. Often it turns out that those concerns are only partly justified.

For instance, that reaching the final is a huge success and that it would just be a bonus to win that as well. Or that it is realistic to assume that I will reach other finals. Thinking of it as a singular event would be too pessimistic.

About "acceptance": When I know the causes of my fears and doubts, it becomes easier to accept them. There are people who worry less and therefore have fewer concerns. But I am one of the overthinkers and have to accept that anxiety and doubt will always be a part of me.

Therefore, I view nervousness, anxiety, and doubt more as a part of a personal challenge that I must overcome, just like physical and tactical challenges.

About "conscious countering": I am proactive in working on my anxiety, nervousness, and doubts and personalize them as, for instance, friends, before and also during my matches. In my mind I anticipate their visit. So, I beat them to it. I'm prepared and have already set an imaginary table.

Next is some brief small talk:

- *Where did you come from?*
- *What do you want to tell me?*

I listen patiently, but then quickly point out that we're in my house and that there is something important I have to do—like, for example, win the final.

Then there are two options: Either I quickly walk them to the door and dismiss them from my thoughts, or they stay and we play the match together, sort of like a team. Personifying emotions is a classic strategy from applied psychology, and while it may sound odd to some people, it works for me.

WILD CARD

Let's take a closer look at anxiety's little sister, **nervousness**. It has a record-setting degree of familiarity. Hardly anyone has never experienced it, at least slightly. And there is barely anyone who doesn't curse it and wishes to be immune from it.

But that is exactly what usually makes it worse. Those who wrangle with their nervousness typically end up in an unpleasant maelstrom. Now it's not just nerves, but also the continuous thinking about one's nervousness that adds to the torment: the thought of being nervous and therefore weak. Anger and annoyance about oneself set in. The result: a negative spiral.

But we can, in fact, tear away the menacing mask of nervousness quite easily. Because often nervousness isn't as bad as it feels.

Step one: We no longer play dumb and recognize that feeling nervous is natural. Understanding it as a normal response that gets in the way of every person in a performance situation as a perceived hurdle is incredibly helpful.

This is automatically followed by step two: We accept our nervousness as a companion that cannot simply be eliminated, similar to default settings on our computer.

And step three also follows automatically: The realization that nervousness isn't some exotic phenomenon and doesn't make me a weak performer.

In step four, we even elevate nervousness and view it as an important sign that an important moment is about to occur: I should be alert, clearheaded, and focused.

Even if after all these steps nervousness is already properly contextualized, in step five I will give it an unburdened but very suitable new name. I turn it into "helpful tension", a term with which I am immediately at peace. Best buddies with my nervousness, what a luxury!

In the past, I was always annoyed with my excessive nervousness before matches. I would have liked to come into the game more chill. I always thought everyone else was so relaxed, just not me.

Then I had a conversation with the sports psychologist on the WTA tour with whom I began to work over the years. She is available to us female players in situ at some of the big tournaments. When she told me that most of the players were extremely nervous before their matches and these types of conversations were the order of the day for her, it changed my appraisal.

Since then, I tell myself: "Don't make yourself less than what you are!" After all, the others struggle with the same problems as you, even if you can't tell on the outside. What matters is who can handle them better.

While this realization didn't make my nervousness disappear, I do handle it differently now. I no longer get upset about it, waste unnecessary energy, but instead try to accept my nerves and ideally even use them to my advantage: as an activator and mainspring, as my body's signal to me that I am ready, and that the impending task is really important to me.

Because one thing I realized is that the worst matches I played over the years were, by far, the ones when I was too relaxed, too positive, too casual.

And finally, different relaxation strategies can, of course, also help us calm down. It can be taking a walk, taking a swim in the lake, enjoying a certain kind of music, taking a bubble bath with essential oils or meeting friends. The list is endless. There are many "lists of pleasant activities"—all based on psychotherapy treatments for depression—which can help identify potential sources of relief during different phases of a depressed mood.

But **relaxation techniques** and **mindfulness exercises** that we develop ourselves are also effective. As previously mentioned, there is evidence that autogenic training, meditation, and breathing techniques are beneficial to coping with anxiety. Even just imagining warmth can stimulate muscles to relax.

However, even with the use of some of these methods, we must remember that the feeling of nervousness is a kind of performance component. "When I wasn't nervous it didn't go well," says Barbara Engleder, the sports shooter who won gold at the 2016 Olympics in Rio de Janeiro. "We need nervousness so we'll be alert." Likewise, Jeff Greenwald quotes basketball legend Michael Jordan: "The day I don't feel nervous is the day I know I must quit the game of basketball."[38]

So, it only works with nervousness. And then he goes on to quote Pete Sampras, the former number one in the tennis world rankings. What does he miss most after ending his career? Apparently, he told the magazine *Inside Tennis* the anxiety that gave him the feeling of having to vomit before the Wimbledon final.

According to Greenwald, "embracing the feeling of pressure" helps. If the athlete is not only able to accept the feeling of pressure but also immediately embrace it, it increases their chances of winning. When we stand with our back to the wall, that's the moment we must stand particularly tall. That is when we must tell ourselves that we love the moment and don't wish to be anywhere else.

CREATING ONE'S OWN VIBE

"You win or lose the game before you even step onto the court." That's how Venus Williams once put it.[39] The quality of time prior to a match counts, well-thought-out preparation is essential. Kobe Bryant described

it like this: "I basically try to feel the energy of that setting and let it flow through me. It stimulates me and fuels my desire to play well."[40]

---

38   Greenwald (2007, pg. 4f).
39   Williams (2020).
40   Bryant (2019, pg. 87).

And that preparation is very personal. There are players who want to relax before a game, quickly get warmed up, eat something, and then they're off to the races. Others spend a long time playing on their cellphone or watch the matches on the big screen in the locker room. And then there are those who like it pretty chill, play cards with their team in the players' lounge, and through a mix of laughter and relaxation try to keep their own activation level where it is not too high but comfortable.

And then there are the meticulous ones like me. Even if the match doesn't start until 8 p.m., we want to gear up the entire day, even the night before, for the perfect match start:

* *What time and what will I eat for dinner?*
* *When do I go to bed?*
* *What will I have for breakfast, lunch?*

A quick power nap after eating, then an extensive warm-up with my coach or sparring partner, a tactical meeting, one more physical therapist treatment for the ideal muscle tone.

The sports drinks are mixed, all the rackets are strung with a different tension, labeled, all grips are newly wrapped in the particular way I like. Not too thick, not too round. The logos have been painted, my bag is packed with everything where I need it, accessible with one reach of the hand.

Everything is prepared for any possible game. I have enough equipment and refreshments for a marathon match. And right before the match: rest—and the comforting certainty that everything is optimally prepared and I'm ready to go.

47

It is always evident that the variety of human personalities necessitates personalized approaches. The method must fit the person. If the speaker on the stage doesn't seem authentic, he can pack up and go home. When the elite athlete doesn't play to his strengths, the likelihood that he will lose increases.

Strategies also frequently need to be adapted, for instance, to age, and here more specifically to the chronological, biological, and training age. The experiences a person has gathered in life, specifically in sport, are an important factor.

The way we find our personal "zone of optimal functioning" changes over time. Just like we, too, change over time. It is worth trying out different strategies, to choose one and then formulate it so it can ultimately be used in very different situations.

Ideally it will all become routine, and each time the process will automatically take its course. The optimal activation level feels like a good mix of anxiety and clarity, of unpredictability and deep faith in one's abilities.

So, it's about generating an emotional level that corresponds to the challenge. The athlete must reach precisely this effective high-performance zone, not accidentally but consciously and in a controlled manner, right from the start. The match-day coordinates must be defined:

- What can be achieved within the scope of today's possibilities? Within the scope of *my* abilities?

- Where do I locate my maximum performance on the x-axis that will lead to maximum success on the y-axis?

Someone who is looking for fulfillment within the realms of what is maximally achievable takes a big risk—the risk of being quickly frustrated with the task of cracking this incredibly high threshold. The fact is that frustration isn't a powerful driver for great performances. Let's be honest, the days when everything or almost everything works out are an exception. Our efforts really pertain to an optimum: our own abilities must be optimized again and again for the here and now.

The imaginary boundaries our daily physical form draws around us must be recognized and, importantly, acknowledged. Golf legend Bernhard Langer, former number one in the golf world rankings and currently the most successful player on the senior tour, uses this idea as a basis to motivate himself. He strives to always bring out the best Bernhard Langer that "the day will allow."[41]

Intending to act prudently, ideally within the scope of current possibilities, might work as a guiding theme for athletic and many other challenges. This strategy means setting that framework early.

A 2021 study completed at the sports college in Cologne, Germany,[42] showed that this endeavor often proliferates into unwanted utopia. *"Mental nicht voll da" ("Mentally not all there")* was written in several German newspapers the day after the study's pre-release. A team of 1,122 athletes sponsored by Deutsche Sporthilfe (German Athletes' Support) had been surveyed. It turned out that three out of ten athletes (male and female) from the Olympic and paralympic team were "mentally not fully present" at the peak of their season. Even among the Olympic finalists, it was still just 24 percent.

This quote is concerning because it puts into question the international competitiveness of our elite sports. But the quote is also concerning because it reveals that mental optimization is not prioritized to the extent that it should be. The study also emphasizes that mental presence is one of the truly most important variables for success in sports.

---

41 Brunner (2020, pg. 51).
42 Deutsche Sporthilfe (2021).

Creating structures, building security

However, these results do not mean that high-performance athletes don't pay sufficient attention to their mental state. There are always functional barriers that turn mental presence into temporary distraction and even absence—because mental strength doesn't simply result from targeted self-talk and relaxation techniques. Many factors come into play here.

Multiple stressors and logistical complexities are problems that should be taken seriously. There are multiple stressors, for instance, because sponsor contracts and the support provided by German Athletes' Support are not enough to make a living, and therefore athletes must also hold down a job. Or those athletes who are not quite elite soccer players, golfers, or tennis players, and so are unable to save enough money for the days after their active career ends, must therefore simultaneously go to college or complete an apprenticeship.

It is therefore important to plan everyday life wisely. A survey of Olympic athletes found that approximately one-third of those questioned had insufficient financial means to fully concentrate on their sport. Thus, having multiple stressors has become society's ugly trend. Statistical analysis reveals that in 2019, 4.1 million people had more than one job. Twenty years ago, it was only 1.8 million.[43]

When money becomes a limiting factor, difficulties such as compromises and restrictions are not far behind. If circumstances allow, it is sensible to look beyond the money at the whole package. Just earning lots of money doesn't satisfy in the long run and inhibits productivity, not to mention the negative effect on creativity.

The total package also matters in work life outside of sports, such as what the job has to offer aside from money.

---

43   Statista Research Department (2020).

- How stressful are the individual processes?

- What about college, my team, my working atmosphere?

Much is predefined, based on the type of sport or the job sector. But it should be understood that we can intervene creatively in some setting structures, especially when it comes to setting major goals. This necessity increases proportionately to the size of the athletic and work goals that have been set.

The new office you are moving into is a mess. So, clean it up. Your study is bleak and cold. Then decorate it in a way that feels good to you. Dissatisfaction can often be sensibly rectified in mundane ways.

We appropriate our environment and generate trust through familiarity, **habituation**, as it is called in expert circles. Home advantage, among other things, feeds on this power. Your own conference room, your own company premises, your own athletic field, soccer field, or tennis court. Familiarity with the home setting helps establish advantage.

We are familiar with every nook, with the acoustics, the light conditions, and the ground condition. The atmosphere in local stadiums and center courts, together with the cheering fans, creates a competitive advantage. Even just thinking about the excited hometown crowd generates a feeling of euphoria. A feeling that one can take advantage

Creating the right vibe on the court is important to me, a kind of flow I create myself by getting into the game right from the start with my own shots, points, and my behavior. I don't want it to be hectic. I want to show up but also want to lay down a marker early on. I soak up positive aspects and ignore negative ones. To me, it's important to feel the vibe on the court and influence it to my advantage.

of beforehand, for instance, by mentally transporting oneself to these supportive scenarios with fans, maybe as a daily, intoxicatingly beneficial visualization exercise.

So, does that mean a competition is most successful on home turf? Scientists took a close look at the achievements of 6,500 international elite soccer players and found that there really is a home advantage. The home team won every other game; the remaining games ended either in a draw or a loss in equal numbers by both teams.[44]

Profiting from home advantage

And doesn't the hosting nation of the Olympics tend to earn disproportionately more medals for their home country? During the 2020 Olympics held in Tokyo in 2021, Japan ended up in third place in the medal count. In 2016 in Rio, Japan came in sixth, and in 2012 in London, only eleventh.

British researchers found that this phenomenon can be traced back to biological causes. With the use of saliva tests, they were able to determine that the testosterone levels of soccer players was significantly higher before a home game than an away game. The researchers found that testosterone plays an important role in various team sports to create that modicum of advantage over the opponent in a home game.[45]

The Olympic Games bring with them additional aspects of activation, especially the enormous importance of a top event and the associated huge media attention, as well as the equally huge expectations, especially from the home crowd. All athletes are familiar with the home game atmosphere and the euphoria that comes with it.

44   Czycholl (2020).
45   Neave & Wolfson (2003).

One good example is my win in Stuttgart, my home game. I beat three top ten players in a row. I had endless self-confidence. And the more success-fully I played, the more everything went according to plan.

- *What would you like room service to bring you for dinner?*
- *What music would you like for your stadium entrance at the semi-finals?*
- *For when and for how long should we reserve the practice court?*

The audience loved me, and that helped me play myself into a kind of rapture. I rode a wave of euphoria during the entire tournament.

But a Belgian team of researchers said "Stop! It's not quite like that with the home advantage." These researchers looked at first-match and return-match configurations of European soccer league and Champions League games between 2010 and 2017. And they looked at whether a team whose second game was a home game had been able to bene-fit from that and possibly able to compensate for a point deficit. That assumption would be reasonable given the possibility of the home crowd having clapped, roared, and carried them to victory.

"We find that playing the second leg of a knock-out confrontation at home is not associated with a substantially higher chance of proceeding to the next stage of the tournament."[46] Meaning: the home advantage is not 100 percent reliable. Nevertheless, there is one compulsory finding: the more I familiarize myself with what is in store, the more familiar it feels and the smaller the risk of a surprise and the distraction that comes with it.

It's different at out-of-town venues. There is the initial effort of confront-ing the unfamiliar gymnasium's sprung floor or the golf course design, far from home. That is precisely why the golfer plays trial rounds before the start of the competition.

46   Amez et al. (2020).

There are some courts we might struggle with. For instance, when we finally get to play on one of the big courts during the advanced portion of the tournament after playing several days on one of the outside courts. Now everything is unfamiliar, everything looks different. There is much more run back and side run-off space, the stands behind the opponent are several meters tall, sometimes there are distracting screens or advertisements that can even make the ball invisible for a brief moment.

When a court makes me uncomfortable, I have to try to gradually make it my own. To generate a good performance, it's important to feel at one with the conditions. Without that harmony, it gets difficult, and the athlete has trouble getting into the match.

When there is the opportunity to play on the same court multiple times, it will feel increasingly familiar over the course of the tournament, and the athlete is prepared. It starts on the way to the court and continues with the now familiar voice of the announcer, who dramatically shouts your name into the microphone as you enter the stadium. And finally, the spectators' applause, which can be very different depending on whether you're a compatriot, a favorite, the underdog, popular, or unpopular.

You are familiar with the bench; you know where to put your bag. You nod to the referee, whom you might already know from another match that week. Everything is in its place, the drinks, the towels. Everything is the way it's been, and particularly in very stressful moments, it is a nice feeling of familiarity. Humans are creatures of habit, especially athletes.

Every tennis match has its own character composed of the court, the match itself, the behavior of the players, the impact of the spectators, various other factors, and, of course, interference factors.

> *On some courts an athlete might feel terrific from the start, the match goes smoothly, and there is a good connection with the court. But sometimes it's the opposite, nothing works, it feels uncomfortable and bumpy throughout the match.*
>
> *My goal when I step onto the court is to create a connection with this day, this court, these conditions. In doing so, it is important to accept what we can't control and what can't be changed. We have to be flexible and adapt.*
>
> *But when we are able to be in accord with the opponent, the court, the weather, the spectators, and all of the other conditions, and can soak up the good and accept what is not so good, then our game can really evolve. It sounds so easy, but it's work in the form of good preparation. Uncertainty and the concomitant loss of control trigger a lot of stress.*

The discussion about home advantage and away disadvantage has been weakened. Opinions, and as we have already seen, even study results can differ. Relying solely on statistics would also not be consistent with mental training control. Because that would mean leaving the decision over winning and losing to external circumstances. This type of heteronomy would not be a viable framework for long-term top performances.

A better approach would be to remove the unfamiliarity from distant competition venues. Unfamiliarity takes up energy because the athlete has to adjust within a short time. This could result in incalculable uncertainty.

That means an effective antidote would be to get familiar with the out-of-town competition venue beforehand. Ideally, the athlete already knows the court, the gym, the water, the terrain, the space, or at least has the opportunity to familiarize themself with everything in situ before the start of the competition.

- *How do I prepare for a location?*
- *Don't I already know this court inside and out?*

If not, I have to familiarize myself with it. In 2016, when I played for the first time at the US Open in the Arthur Ashe Stadium at Flushing Meadows in front of a capacity crowd, the biggest tennis stadium in the world, in a night-session match against Kvitova, I had already booked a morning training session on the court. Early in the morning when the stadium was still empty and no games had been scheduled, the stadium was mine and it was peaceful.

I imagined 10,000 fans sitting in the stands, cheering, possibly making noise between points, or shouting down to the court. In between my practice serves, I visualized what the colorful crowd of spectators in the background, the line judges, and the ball boys would look like.

While sitting on the bench, I imagined how the advertising banners surrounding the court would light up, how the ads would flicker across them, and loud music would accompany the change of ends. I visualized all of these things. And when I stepped onto the court that night to play the match, many things were as I had imagined them. It was a good feeling.

Of course, the actual court experience can never be completely simulated. We always have to anticipate the unexpected interfering with the imaginable. Every space and every impending experience in that space has its own character.

Familiar, unfamiliar, and neutral locations also play a role in other life contexts. I would much rather have a tough negotiation take place in my own office than on the contractual partner's turf. Our own four walls give us certainty. The unknown remains outside; I can reduce my preparation efforts to what matters: the content.

As previously mentioned, golfers are among the best preparation strategists. They travel to the venue days before the tournament begins to play several practice rounds on the course and write down detailed information about each hole.

The "birdie books" in which they record this strategically important information, are in themselves a neatly measured grid of the course. They then add personal comments, findings regarding the undulation of the Green, all the way to highly technical playing strategies, etc.

"I think I always prepared a little better than the others", said Bernhard Langer. "When I play a course for the first time, I like to play it alone so I am not distracted by other players. I really want to see everything I need to see on the course, where I want and don't want to hit the ball."[47]

Golf courses might be more different from each other than strung floors in a gym or tennis sand. But there are still differences there. And the more unpredictability we can remove from these differences, the more we deprive them of their irritating power. One way to do so is to frequently play on unfamiliar courts during training phases, even just to make the feeling of encountering something new ordinary.

PREPARING FOR THE UNEXPECTED

Uncertainty, loss of control, stress. Sports psychologists Anna-Maria Elbe and Jürgen Beckmann refer to a "negative emotional state with undirected activation,"[48] under which ease and movement coordination and, ultimately, the ability to compete, suffer. The ability to realistically classify impending challenges and meet them in a thoughtful and performance-oriented way is lost.

Sometimes the feeling of uncertainly changes to anxiety. As we already mentioned, anxiety is disruptive, paralyzing. As previously mentioned, that is why Elbe and Beckmann recommend reframing anxiety as fear.

---

47   Brunner (2020, pg. 48).
48   Beckmann & Elbe (2008, pg. 119).

> *Being able to assess pressure situations before-hand, to know as accurately as possible what will happen—and this is very important—to know the strategies one has at one's disposal, is extremely valuable to one's ability to respond confidently.*
>
> *Hence a good performance is typically based on very good preparation as well as a good amount of flexibility to be able to appropriately respond to very different situations.*

Surprises, to the extent that we even want to allow ourselves to classify them as such, are part of the whole thing, and our flexibility determines how we will handle them. But even if we anticipate only 80 percent or 50 percent, or even just 10 percent, that's 80, 50, or 10 percent less unexpected stress, and that leaves us more capacity for dealing with the actual task at hand. That can be the tennis match, but also a presentation, a job interview, and any number of other challenging life tasks in the private as well as the professional sphere.

Thinking of something new as a friend who occasionally surprises us with something unexpected is very effective. And we want to add another friend to this clique of easy-going friends: the awareness and understanding that not everything out there can be controlled and that control cannot be forced.

Carsten Arriens, former head of the Davis-Cup team and Jan-Lennard Strüff's coach, describes what happens when he senses in the morning that something is wrong with the athlete. "If my expert knowledge was all I had was to work with on those days, I would not get very far."[49] Not everything can be measured by traditional standards, no two days are alike.

---

49   Memmert & Leiner (2020, pg. 12).

That's how it was at the aforementioned night match at Flushing Meadows. A lot happened the way I had anticipated. But some things were different. The light was much brighter than expected. The packed stands made everything seem even bigger. And it was much louder than I could have imagined!

The entire stadium seemed to roar, even at moments when no one was yelling or applauding. It was a continuous noise that made it difficult to relax on the bench during the changes of ends.

It would be an illusion to think everything would go according to plan. That doesn't happen 99 percent of the time. The reality, which sets in long before the first service, often deviates.

For instance, the preparation might not have been ideal in spite of all the meticulousness. Maybe you couldn't get to sleep the night before, or maybe the trash truck clattered in front of the hotel at six in the morning and tore you from the sleep that is so essential to regeneration. Maybe that training court at Arthur Ashe or the warm-up court where you warmed up before all the other matches weren't available. Or you didn't have your winner shirt, the top you wore during all your other victories, but this time it didn't make it back from the laundry service in time.

"The shirt? What, it's not here?!" Then you send one of the team members to find it. In the end, you might have to work without the winner's shirt. And you're not going to lose because of a dumb shirt! The match in question didn't go as I had wished, but I felt like I had prepared as well as possible.

US Open 2016: ice to be able to manage the unpredictable with a cool head.

© picture alliance, Ray Stubblebine, dpa

Disruptions must be tolerated. Better yet: change the function of the disruption. What was previously viewed as a disruption now becomes a kind of companion or one of everyday life's shenanigans. I might dislike the trash truck's racket at dawn, but I cannot let it affect me. The association chain of noise-annoying-interferes-impairs-weakens must be severed.

A change of perspective would trigger very different associations. Possibly regret that the sanitation workers have to work so hard that early in the morning. The noise would most likely still cause me to lose sleep, but I won't allow this racket to irritate me and thereby waste important energy before I have even gotten out of bed.

Certainly, the ability to not allow oneself to be distracted by irrelevant information, not to get worked up, to be able to decide and act spontaneously, and thereby be able to tap into one's full repertoire is one of the most important qualities of champions. That is particularly true when being confronted with unpleasant and unexpected situations.

And then the pandemic happened and with it the most unexpected thing of all. The sport collapsed. Leagues were suspended, major tournaments were postponed, even the Olympic Games were moved to a different year. 2010, 2014, 2016, 2021—until recently no one would have thought such a time sequence would be correct. Then came the phase of a match schedule that was only reliable after the games had already been played. Covid caused last-minute cancelations. Or changes to a team's lineup and formation.

In January 2022, FC Bayern Munich was missing nine players, endangering the start of the second half of the season. Nine Covid-positive players were also missing from the German national handball team during the third European Championships game against Poland on January 18, of the same year. And it got worse.

WILD CARD

All of this did not only weaken the affected teams but also caused lots of uncertainty. Additionally, everyone anxiously waited for new positive cases to be reported, which resulted in even more degradation, changes in game strategy, and general insecurities. And athletic comparability also quickly takes a backseat when victory and defeat are determined by the number of sick and infected players instead of playing ability.

And regularly held matches were sometimes not matches under familiar normal conditions. Sometimes only half the number of spectators was allowed, other times only a quarter, 10 percent, or none. The stadiums echoed like they do during training sessions. The stands were silent as though there was nothing to cheer for. In this particular case, it was impossible to prepare for the unexpected. At least not at the beginning of the pandemic.

When we had to play in front of empty backdrops, I realized what really attracted me to playing tournaments. It's the thrill, the atmosphere on the court, the suspense, the fans' reactions when they are completely quiet before a big point followed by thunderous applause after a good rally. I missed all of that during the pandemic. I became aware of how much I had taken it for granted to stand in the spotlight before the fans and the television cameras.

When things started up again, at least without spectators, after the tournament break, I felt primarily euphoria. I was just happy to play tournaments again. Getting motivated wasn't hard. But with each additional week without the spectators and the vibe, finding a good tension level during matches became more difficult. The adrenaline just wasn't there.

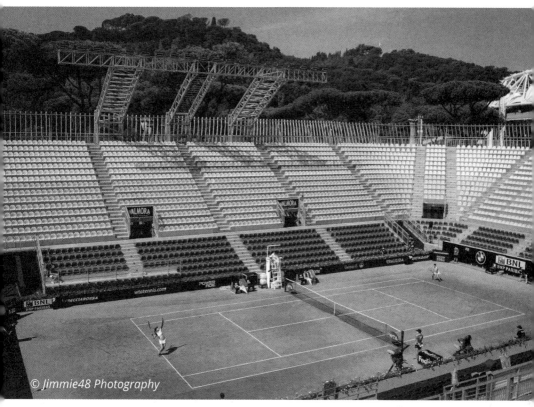
© Jimmie48 Photography

Consequences of the pandemic: When top-level tournament matches feel like training games.

The pandemic defined and limited the range of movement. Hotel, tennis court, hotel, tennis court, a humiliating endless loop. There were also forced time constraints—early arrival was absolutely essential to accommodate PCR tests and quarantine. It was a tight schedule. Spending an hour just being a person or a tourist was no longer possible.

It can be said that everyone had to equally bow to the rules, meaning no one was favored or disadvantaged. But players who tend to focus on more than just tennis would have felt the restrictive measures or reprimands more keenly.

Since all activity was limited to the tennis stadium and the hotel, we ended up training even more than usual. But more doesn't always yield more. To me the fact that my personal focus was confined to my work felt more like a burden.

Because ordinarily, at tournaments, it was always important to me to make free time for experiences that have nothing to do with tennis. When I spend all year flying from one tournament to another and am constantly around my competition at the tennis stadiums and hotels, it is downright refreshing and really important for the psyche to occasionally do and see something different and be around other people.

I have always tried to disconnect from the tennis circus, at least occasionally, to be able to think about the next match in a tennis-free setting.

The tennis restrictions resulting from Covid measures represent a very specific category of mental tasks.

- **Challenge level 1:** Accepting things that cannot be changed.

- **Challenge level 2:** Understanding that frustration and anger would severely impact vital energy.

- **Challenge level 3:** Being able to draw satisfaction from the knowledge that one is a professional and thus capable of accepting unpleasant things. Those unpleasant things include having to complete one's fitness program in a hotel room with the windows open.

GETTING TO KNOW THE OPPONENT

Another basic component of preparation is the opponent analysis. In sports, just as in life in general, this can be one person, a group of people, or an entire team. In elite sports we make use of the analysis that makes tactical, individual, and play-related details about the opponent transparent, if necessary, in super-slow motion and as freeze frame images.

And to take away power from any remaining unknowns, I can also face uncomfortable as well as unfamiliar training opponents during preparation.

I treat the opponent like I treat the environmental conditions: I try to analyze them beforehand so I can get a sense of what to expect. On the one hand, to be able to produce a good performance, but on the other hand, to mentally fortify myself so I can come to the match full of self-confidence. Good preparation calms the nerves.

The way I adapt to an opponent usually begins with an analysis of her game, preferably live if she has a prior match. But it can also be via a video analysis of earlier games.

Another option is talking to other players, coaches, and external experts to find out how they assess this opponent's play and what ideas they might have to counter it. Together with my team, I thereby develop a roadmap for my playing strategy in the match against her.

Many players on the tour have a rigid playing style. Their goal is to force their game on the opponent. It is what they learned and practiced from a young age.

Of course, everyone has a certain playing style and sometimes only one game strategy. But that one strategy can be enough. Because when someone, for instance, plays so fast and so aggressive that it puts me under constant pressure, all my knowledge about their defensive running weaknesses doesn't help me very much. I don't even get a chance to exploit that knowledge.

By the way, it can become a particular mental challenge when I am brought to my knees with this strategy, even though I would possibly keep the upper hand in all other requirements.

Having barely perceptible weaknesses and being able to, if necessary, cleverly adapt to the match situation and the opponents is, of course, a quality of particularly good players.

I have always been the type to take my cue from my opponent while focusing on trying to disrupt her game as much as possible. Others consider this intensive engagement of the opponent as stressful. They claim that it puts them off their own game. This topic must certainly also be viewed through the lens of individual preferences.

It is apparent that with all the value ascribed to spontaneity and intuition, the fact is that the more details we can anticipate about a competition, the better we are able to prepare, which, on the one hand, reinforces inner calm and confidence, and on the other hand, also makes preparation for the competition more effective.

Prior to the 2007 World Championships, Henning Fritz, 2004 World Handball Player of the Year studied images of the opponent's throwing style. "I visualized the opponent's throwing images with affirmations, every opposing position. On the evening before the game and again right before the game." He says it gave him certainty. Little by little that inner calm transferred to the quality of his game at the World Championships.

The much more likely *anxiety* that should have occurred due to the circumstances didn't happen. At that time, Fritz was only the third pick at his club, THW Kiel.

He therefore lacked game practice and then was supposed to, out of nowhere, bring a world-level performance as a first pick by national team coach Heiner Brand. He brought it and the World Championships went down in the history books of German handball as a legendary winter fairytale.

For some time now, video analysis has been an effective method not only for getting to know the opponent but to downright study him, at the amateur level as well as the elite club. The successful soccer coach Ralf Rangnick is said to have meticulously penetrated the depths of the opposing top team's strategies via moving image. Paired with statistical as well as his own knowledge, he earned the often-noticeable advantage on the pitch.

It means being familiar with the opponent before a match—his patterns, his balance, his physical, cognitive, and mental strengths. To ideally surprise him because you know him better than he anticipated. Intensive preparation is effective against the opponent, particularly in one-on-one situations where an athlete engages in direct tackles, such as, for instance, in ice hockey or handball, but especially in all forms of martial arts.

Playing with the surprise factor

It is the effect the late talk show host Roger Willemsen created in his interviews. His dialogue partners were always stunned by Willemsen's detailed knowledge about his guests. "How did you know that?" The effect was enormous. The interviewee felt like he was important and taken seriously.

And the sports opponent? He feels threatened and is about to be beaten with his own arsenal. I only have to send the correct signals, verbally and physically. There should be no doubt about my certainty of winning.

The opponent also feels bad when he is demonstrably demoted to a *player with weaknesses*. For instance, this often visibly happens in beach volleyball. The player I target with my serve knows that I either view him as the weaker serve-receive player of his two-man team because it is *he* who now has to safely receive the ball, or that I have identified him as the weaker offensive player, because *he* will again be the player to take offensive action when his partner sets the ball for the attack after receiving the serve.

Worst-case scenario, the player will feel stigmatized as the weak one in both techniques simultaneously: serve-receive and offense. Of course, it must be assumed that both players of a beach volleyball team are familiar with their roles and strength-weakness distribution and are therefore immune to the aforementioned surprises. But it still builds pressure to always take on the responsible part of the serve-receive when the ball arrives with the message that one's technique is not convincing.

When confirming that assumption with serve-receive errors, it not only makes the opponent stronger but also makes the affected person increasingly insecure. A spiral that brings joy only to the serving side.

And then there is that special opponent, the **nemesis**. When you are able to minimize him, show his weaknesses and thereby humanize him, you, of course, take away his power.

Everyone has at least one nemesis—that one player they dread facing in a match and struggle to defeat. That's because we find some player types more disagreeable than others. Their style of play is particularly bothersome or their demeanor is irritating.

There are those specific opponents that make our heart sink, even when they're just in the tournament bracket's proximity. They remind us of painful losses we wish to never experience again, or of such a tough fight, a drawn-out, dogged struggle, that even just thinking about it causes a feeling of intense dread.

The best strategy against this type of opponent is to turn it into a personal challenge I want to confront. So, it's not about who is on the other side of the net, but about me and my development.

Sometimes we make critical progress, particularly when we face the most unpleasant challenges and master them. It makes us grow, and we learn more about ourselves than in most other situations.

There is much too much prognosticating and philosophizing about personal constellations. Player A beat player B and player C, and then loses against player D. Such mind games are pointless and only distract.

In 2016, I played against Serena Williams in the second round at Indian Wells. I heard so much about her in the run-up, about her strengths and which aspects of her game I had to absolutely look out for. I had planned to shoot for the moon in this match, but I was also very nervous.

The match went unsung for me with a 2:6 and 1:6 loss. I had so much respect for her that I lost more so against her name and her myth, than the person.

Ever since that match, I try to remain as objective as possible in my head. Everyone has their daily form, even the very best. It's all about being better than your opponent on this day and in this match.

David did it against Goliath. There are many examples of not-so-athletic Davids bringing super-athletic Goliaths to their knees. For instance, let's take a look at the US national soccer team at the 1950 World Cup in Brazil. They shot the heavily favored English team right out of the tournament with a 1:0 win. The winning goal was scored by Josef Gaetjens, a student. Prior to the match, the odds were 1:500.[50] It can be done!

Even the renowned sports psychologist Lothar Linz refers to the historical David as someone with good qualifications, which, when combined,

---

50   Neue Szene (2018).

were decisive in his success. They can be seen in his fight against Goliath: David was courageous, confident of victory, merciless, aware of his strengths and used them, acted suddenly and first.[51] These attributes would look good on anyone who really wants to win.

The underdog doesn't assimilate all attributes from the start. A few can be planned, regardless of the external circumstances. Mercilessness, which in this context has nothing to do with brutality, is a sports-related precept that can be aspired to. And everyone should already know and use their strengths and then use the element of surprise as an effective strategy that can be deployed, particularly when one acts faster than the opponent.

Using all of this as a basis creates a foundation for a courageous performance. Whether it will also result in the certainty of winning is anyone's guess. But you must believe that a surprise victory is possible.

A very different and also promising strategy that is at least worth considering is to make oneself the nemesis of others. The possibilities of doing so in sports are almost certainly limited because our actions should be consistent and reflect who we are. Serving underhand and through the legs at that, as Nick Kyrgios regularly did successfully, is not everyone's cup of tea.

The options are broader in our working life. And we don't have to try and scare everyone. We would have also scored if we elicited a nod of recognition from the opponent. The element of surprise is a tried-and-proven method. It works everywhere, in a movie, in a newspaper article, in a résumé, or in any type of stage performance.

The element of surprise not only breaks up monotony and boredom but also manages to stand out from the lively surrounding circumstances. Does anything speak against enriching each of our performances with at least one surprising moment? Surprises are memorable. Not having anticipated something enriching and still receiving it, is a gift.

---

51 Linz (2014, pg. 169).

SUMMARY

Finding your own ideal pre-start condition, coping with anxiety and nervousness, and optimally preparing yourself for an impending task are abilities that require experience, patience, and sensitivity, with each one involving a very different approach.

GETTING INTO THE GAME

Drawing on good experiences *** using music *** meditating *** using relaxation techniques *** withdrawing *** looking to talk with someone *** getting psyched up.

TEACHING ANXIETY TO BE AFRAID

Acceptance *** knowing my boundaries *** systematic desensitization *** differentiating between anxiety and fearfulness *** differentiating causes *** reinterpreting anxiety *** nervousness as a friend and activation assistant *** changing perspectives *** using lists of pleasant activities.

CREATING ONE'S OWN VIBE

Accepting form of the day as a factor *** optimum instead of perfection *** giving what is possible at the moment *** soaking up positive aspects, ignoring negative ones *** anticipating visualization exercises *** getting familiar with competitive sports.

PREPARING FOR THE UNEXPECTED

Accepting disruptions *** reinterpreting disruptions *** changing perspectives *** finding satisfaction in my own professional response.

GETTING TO KNOW THE OPPONENT

Video analyses *** talking to other players and experts *** visualizing scenarios with affirmations *** bringing the element of surprise *** exuding the desire to win *** minimizing nemeses and demonstrating their weaknesses.

2

The match picks up pace

© picture alliance, Bernd Weißbrod, dpa

BREAK AND REBREAK: BEING IN THE FLOW

Serotonin, dopamine, and noradrenaline—they are jokers in our system: the happiness hormones. We must nurture them and keep them happy. And science tells us how to do so by providing us with happiness-hormone boosters: chocolate, for instance, which is only mentioned here but not elaborated on for obvious reasons. Another happiness-hormone accelerator is much more important: movement or sport, which can help us find happiness or, at least, happy moments.

Let's take serotonin. It regulates our satisfaction gauge. When there is a sufficient amount, it binds to receptors in the brain and writes a feel-good program in the control center. We feel motivated, our mood lifts. Sports give us those moments of hormone release, not just during the glorious moment of a win, but also along the way. And on top of that, when sport is done for its own sake, we feel free of rules and goals.

- What happens to us and inside us when we are overcome by joy?

- Why does the unexpected and impressive Olympic win make us emotional?

- Why do people cry when they cross the finish line at a marathon for the very first time?

Christian Kreienbühl has conclusive answers. The two-hour-and-thirteen-minutes runner was a member of the Swiss national team, and he and his team won third and fourth place at the European Track and Field Championships in 2014 and 2018, respectively.

What are those final kilometers before the finish line like? "It's like being a child and running barefoot down a grassy slope, knowing that your favorite ice cream is waiting for you at the bottom of the hill."[52] And when things go really well, such as when Kreienbühl won bronze at the European Championships, "then you might experience one of the most beautiful things that can happen to someone in life: crying tears of joy."

---

52 Kreienbühl (2018)

What the European championship is to this Swiss national team runner is what the New York Marathon is to the ambitious recreational athlete. At this world-renowned race, the locals line the streets in Central Park, and they even stand several rows deep for the final kilometer on both sides. The runners and their fans don't know each other, yet they feel close, spatially and emotionally.

The "Go, go, go!" from the spectators carries the runners across the finish line. Happiness hormones flow through the body, and potentially do so for some time. Kreienbühl tells us that his "high" lasts for two to three weeks. "During that time, I practically fly through my daily routine. Many things seem incredibly easy."[53]

UNDERSTANDING THE MATCH

We can spur ourselves on, motivate ourselves, achieve highs and states of flow. It would be unfortunate and very limiting to always tie our feeling of happiness exclusively to the sense of always having to be better than the others. Because the basic concept of competition only admits very few to its winner circle.

This concept can be distilled down to a very short formula: one wins, one loses. Or slightly more differentiated: the first one wins, the second and third also win a little bit, and everyone else loses. And in some sports, even third place isn't worth anything. Like tennis. So, it's about a very few first places that the confusingly large horde of success-hungry athletes vie for. In other words: There are very few winners and an awful lot of losers.

That's pretty frustrating for the non-winners, especially considering the fact that there is not much fluctuation in the group of winners, meaning it is often the same ones that raise the trophy, the Messis and Ronaldos,

53   Ibid.

the Williamses, Woods, Bolts, Bradys, Gretzkys, Neuners, Grafs, and Halmichs. Changes on the winner's podium often only occur when those who led for years slowly decline due to age.

It's like the worldwide distribution of money. At the end of 2020, about 1 percent of the world's population owned almost half of all the money in the world.[54] This means that very few reap the fruit of their labor, in society overall and especially in the sports market segment. Beyond dispute: it's the sport that makes it so difficult to get all the way to the top, and that ultimately the hope for success is greater than any rational forecast.

It is not a philosophical digression on the overrated question of fairness. Rather, it is about generating more satisfaction, or better yet, producing more satisfied individuals from this blatant disproportion. Or simply put:

* How can an ambitious, diligent person, and particularly a hard-working, talented athlete also find some personal gratification off the winner's podium?

Meaning, equating satisfaction solely with the number of victories—with such a low chance of winning—is more than precarious. While winning might be a person's ultimate goal, the journey is also of value. The arrangement must be mutually agreeable, which is also something employers and employees say when they negotiate salaries.

So, it's not just about the salary deposited into your account at the end of the month meeting your demand. The four weeks prior to payday are also of value. This corporate concept also applies in sports and can be projected onto a match, a tournament, a season, or even an athlete's entire sports career.

Hence, we need to think about the demands and desires with which we approach our goals. And, whether sports or athletics, it is primarily not

---

54   Statista Research Department (2022d).

a question of physics, but of the psyche, which organizes the system that is human as a facilitator and regulator, much like a traffic- and information network.

That's how Paul Kunath, who established and headed the department of sports psychology at the prestigious German College of Physical Culture in Leipzig in 1961, eloquently described it.[55] We must think about what it is we want in terms of our long- and short-term goals.

Win or loss. Good or bad match. Healthy or injured. Only striving for perfection, considering only the best as good enough and, if necessary, forcing it; for years, these things prevented me from tapping my full potential. And it mostly kept me from enjoying the small steps. My greatest developmental leaps forward only came when I was finally able to stop seeing everything as black or white.

It was particularly evident in my younger years; everything had to be perfect. The preparation, training, the match. Every dent in my performance or inconsistency in the process on the way to my goal felt like something unwanted, something bad. On my quest for perfection, I was nearly always disappointed. One thing is certain: the ideal of perfection is a rarity, and not only in professional sports.

My delusion regarding perfection even caused me to completely lose my joy in playing tennis, and for a while I did not play professional tennis at all. My view of perfection, performance, and success changed a lot during my hiatus.

I learned to look at my career as a whole, but also view my matches as small journeys, with their highs and lows, with which I wanted to consciously engage. With that attitude in the back of my head, I was able to play a very different kind of tennis. I still had a goal, but a different one.

---

55   Eberspächer (2012, pg. 15).

WILD CARD

Viewing our own performance and development as small stages in a journey can become a worthwhile goal and can underpin the creative process with even more meaning and satisfaction. To that end, working with everyday metaphors always proves an effective vehicle. It transports us through familiar surroundings in our imagination.

Travel is a particularly suitable parallel universe when it comes to process structure. We can accelerate when it is urgent, for instance, when the final minutes of a match must force a decision. And we decelerate when we wish to break up the rhythm or want to buy time.

And when the opponent is setting the pace? We adapt the metaphor accordingly: we briefly become the passenger and wait for the moment when we can retake control of the car to continue the trip in the direction we wish to travel.

We are essentially determined to gain the upper hand as quickly as possible. We try to dominate the rallies from the start, but also the pace and the time between rallies to control the overall atmosphere on the court, to put our own mark on the match. The opponent should feel like it's not her match, not her court, not her day.

On the professional level, there is no time to wait and see how the game evolves. We get down to business immediately, and anyone who can't keep up usually loses.

In tennis you can lose against the opponent or against yourself. In a match there can be phases when you sense that the opponent is getting on the wrong track and having trouble with her own game, for instance, if she starts to hit too hard and makes unforced errors. In moments like these, it can be wise to ride the wave of the match dynamics, for example, to consciously become the passenger with little active intervention.

In doing so, one can, for instance, take a small step back from their own offensive style of play and deliberately return more balls with less speed to entice the opponent to play even more balls with too much power. However, it is important to choose the right moment.

But first you have to become active again and take the wheel as soon as she begins to find solutions. Here the danger is not being able to switch over fast enough to return to your own offensive play. The switch from passenger to driver isn't easy and requires practice.

Handling external influences sensibly

The tempo isn't just set and varied by the players, but also by the coaches, teammates, and referees. Fans can also have a major influence by heckling in quiet moments of intense concentration, whistling, boo-ing, but also with rhythmic chants of encouragement, or sitting behind the basket during the opposing free throw and wildly gesticulating. Whichever direction the irritation or support may go, the athlete must learn to ignore the signals, accept them, or use them as an accompany-ing effect and continue to move to their own rhythm.

Not everyone needs frenetic applause to function well. Some can be invigorated by the headwind. "We always get those not-so-good vibes, for instance, from our competitors," shares Magdalena Neuner. And, of course, it's not just the opposing fans and teams that add pressure by trying to break the athletes' concentration.

Anticipation also generates pressure. Here it is best to follow the sports psychologist Jeff Greenwald and his recommendation to "find pleasure in pressure."[56]

---

56   Greenwald (2007, pg. 4).

In 2017, I was up against the French player Kristina Mladenovic in the final at the Porsche Tennis Grand Prix in Stuttgart. The score was 6:1, 2:6, and 5:4, when I served at match point. At that point, I had played nine hours of clay court tennis and won four matches, three of them against top ten players Svetlana Kuznetsova, Karolina Pliskova, and Simona Halep.

I didn't know if the pressure from the home crowd, who, of course, wanted to see me win, was greater than the pressure I put on myself. The year before, I lost at that same point against Angelique Kerber in the final, when in the eighth match in a week—seven singles and one double—I lacked the strength to win against a top player like her.

Back then, too, I was able to beat several top ten players, but also had to go through the long qualifying process and thus had played two more matches than this time.

So, it's another final. To be honest, I hadn't expected to get another chance to win this prestigious home tournament. Hence, I wanted the win all the more. It was a good match, a very close third set, the outcome completely open.

I had the advantage of being able to serve match point. I tried to keep my mind from drifting neither to the future nor the past, but to stay in the moment, to focus on that next point.

When the score was at a critical 15:30, the chair umpire gave me a time penalty because, in her estimation, I had repeatedly been too slow between points. According to the rules, the time limit between rallies is twenty-five seconds. But at that time, it was at the referees' discretion how scrupulously they wanted to observe this rule and how severely they wanted to punish violations.

To intervene in such a way during this precarious phase of the match was surprising and caused the spectators in the stadium to protest loudly. Catcalls and boos rained down, center court shook.

The score was 15:40, and there is a strong probability that my opponent would break, and due to the equalizer, at 5:5, the match would be wide open again.

Even I was appalled for a moment when the umpire announced the new score. How could she be so insensitive to intervene in the final match at such a tight moment when nerves are raw?! So, I walked over to try and talk to her.

On the way over, many thoughts raced through my head:
- *Why is she doing this to me?*
- *Does fate want me to lose the final yet again?*
- *Was the inappropriate but possibly correct decision a broad hint?*
- *Am I just not meant to win here in Stuttgart?*

I started to feel profound doubt.

And then something incredible happened, which I will never forget. It was a kind of mind shift. I suddenly realized that this umpire call, this small detail, should not have such a major effect on me. That realization came from the bottom of my heart.

I had worked so hard to get to this point in my career, made sacrifices and dealt with disappointments. And now I stood on the center court to give it my all and win.

Could I change the umpire's call? No. Should this call—justified or not—affect my game moving forward? No! The match was tied. Even at a 5:5 score, my chances of winning were as good as my opponent's.

I wasted no more time thinking about the point deduction. It was out of my control and effectively in the past. Nothing but my opponent would keep me from winning. I missed my serve. But I felt strong, and my mind was more focused than ever before. We went on to a tiebreak which, after a 1:4 deficit, I was able to win with a score of 7:5.

© picture alliance, Bernd Weißbrod, dpa

Stuttgart 2017: Learning to accept dubious umpire decisions and shifting the focus to what is controllable.

Reacting appropriately in different situations is challenging. Often, there is no time for strategic considerations, decisions must be made spontaneously, often within seconds. The lucky ones have had similar experiences before and were able to try out possibly different behavior patterns. Also helpful are simple techniques that help us break down situations.

For instance, the situation when an athlete feels he is being treated unfairly by the referee—is it worth a debate, or even getting all worked up?

We are all familiar with this scene from soccer: The referee calls a foul and a wildly gesticulating, dissatisfied crowd runs up to the referee to implore him that everything happened differently and that there is no alternative but to quickly reverse the call. But, no matter how loudly, how vehemently, how assertively the criticism is presented, referees are unlikely to reverse their decisions unless the external VAR referee recommends it. A wild, highly prejudiced crowd cannot do influence the referee.

Such theatrical protests can be simply dismissed as a waste of time and energy. Breaking down the sphere of influence beforehand would be very helpful. The very simple as well as practical three-question technique can be extremely helpful here:

When confronted with a problem, we ask ourselves

Question number one: Is there anything I can do to change it? "Yes," then I will of course change it. "No," I move on to

Question number two: Is there a lesson here? "Yes," I name it and feel like I gained something. "No," then the situation should be crossed off or mentally stored to be dealt with later. And if none of this works, I move on to

Question number three: How do I want this to affect me? The immediate and unanimous response is: I don't want it to affect me! Ideally, that would settle it or should at least take the edge off the situation.

Here, too, I would like to emphasize that we will not always have 100-percent solutions to everything. Instead, we should be glad for every single percentage point that lets us weaken a problem. At the very top level, even one seemingly laughable percentage point can be the difference between victory and defeat. And that brings us back to the many losers who would have loved to occupy one of the few winners' places.

We should also not accept the position of loser—consider, for instance, this decidedly frequent occurrence in everyday life. An intersection, two cars, I do everything right, but the other driver doesn't observe my right of way. Most of the time the situation resolves without an accident.

So, nothing happened, but you're annoyed. You swear, wave your hands about. It's an intense moment and you dwell on it for several more minutes in the car, and even after you get home, you curse: "What an idiot!"

So, he did it, he caused you to behave like an idiot yourself. It wasn't enough that the other guy ignored your right of way and created a dangerous situation. And now he is still dominating your thoughts. Do we really want to allow such a circumstance to have that much influence on us? And it's not just about influence but also an attack on our disposition.

Making our own decisions

The behavior of others affects my safe space, which I should have control over. To Jonas Deichmann, an extreme athlete from Munich, this control is a form of **autonomy**, which is an important part of a successful competition. "Everyone has experienced being in control of the own actions, the master of one's destiny, instead of being pushed around by anonymous powers," says the happiness researcher Mihaly Csikszentmihalyi. During these rare instances, we have a sense of euphoria and deep joy that lasts for a long time and becomes the benchmark of what life should be like."[57]

And, as the extreme athlete Deichmann said in an interview with the German daily newspaper *Süddeutsche Zeitung*[58] in early December 2021, to him, autonomy means freedom. The numbers are convincing evidence of the type of freedom it awakens: The then-thirty-four-year-old spent fourteen months running, cycling, and swimming his way around the world, and he circled the globe over approximately 120 Ironman distances. Autonomy as the fertile substrate for performance, which here almost certainly corresponds to Deichmann's **perceived self-efficacy**, the "subjective belief that one is able to influence the pursuit and realization of goals with one's behavior."[59]

And it is more than mere candor regarding the platitude of being the architect of one's own fortune. It is about giving oneself over to one's vision, a pact with one's own goals. The industrial and cognitive psychologist

---

57 Csikszentmihalyi (2017, pg. 17f.).
58 Regel (2021).
59 Müsseler & Rieger (2017, pg. 245).

Jochen Müsseler and the experimental psychologist Martina Rieger describe it as one of the "best predictors of goal realization."[60]

Doing so requires self-positioning:

- Where do I stand?
- Where do I want to go?

That's when the belief in self-efficacy, which must overcome the actual state to set course for the target state with motivation, comes back into play.

In the same way, Barbara Engleder successfully implemented it before her Olympic victory for Germany in sports shooting. "I constantly self-talk to self-regulate: 'Barbara, you're not here because of the national team, and not because of your family, but because you wanted to be here. You worked toward this moment for twenty years. And that's also why you can decide how it's going to go today.'"

THE POWER OF MOTIVATION

Klay Thompson had to wait 941 days until he was, once again, able to throw baskets for the Golden State Warriors in 2022. A torn ACL immediately followed by a torn Achilles tendon had kept him on sick leave for more than two years. The thirty-one-year-old NBA player scored seventeen points at this first game, back as if nothing had happened.

Even before his injury, Thompson impressed with 40 percent shooting accuracy. He is the NBA's king of three-pointers and holds the record with fourteen three-point shots in a single game.

But his true record is much more than crunching numbers: Klay Thompson believed in his comeback, unceasingly and for an astonishing period of time. While some faltered after just a few months of an injury layoff, Thompson waited patiently for 941 days.

---

60   Ibidem., pg. 242, cited Brunstein (1993, pg. 1061–1070).

WILD CARD

The story speaks for itself. Having a vision and firmly believing in something can strengthen a person, can be incredibly motivating, and can be accompanied by emotional and mental resilience. Michael Steinbach's poignant story illustrates this correlation. The 1992 Olympic quad-scull rowing champion also deserved a gold medal for his ability to effectively visualize his goals:

I remember well the 1976 Winter Olympics in Innsbruck. I sat in front of the TV for hours with my grandfather, watched competitions and admired athletes like skiing stars Franz Klammer and Rosi Mittermaier. Even then, as a six-year-old, I wished to be an Olympic champion someday.

My first success in rowing came in 1985. Second place in single scull at the U16 championships. At that time, I figured that in seven years I could be ready to participate in the 1992 Olympics in Barcelona.

From that moment on, I imagined the Olympic final over and over again during cool-down rowing or on the ergometer after strength training, and in my mind saw myself crossing the finish line first, imagined that success countless times.

In the spring of 1987, I skipped a school field trip to Berlin to attend a preparatory training camp for the Junior World Championships. Shortly afterwards, my classmate Astrid sat next to me on the school bus and asked if it was worth it to skip the field trip for a sport. I assured her that it was definitely worth it, and that she should turn on her TV in August 1992, to watch me become Olympic champion. We wagered a Black Forest cake.

Five years later, I had just returned from Barcelona, when Astrid came to my door with a homemade Black Forest cake.

Explaining this story requires lots of sports psychology vocabulary. These are the things that make a top performer: having a **vision**, setting **goals**, believing in oneself, having the volition to remain motivated long term. Furthermore, there is the fundamental interplay between the individual motive and the situational appeal.[61] Does this mean that with the appropriate amount of commitment I will achieve something that is particularly important to me b?

To me, one of the greatest sources of motivation in sports as well as in life is improving myself, to never stop, to always try something new, and that also brings me joy.

It helps that I am a perfectionist who continuously strives for self-improvement, but also someone who is always searching, who is curious, and who always wants to see the bigger picture. We can learn from other people and other things, and integrate what we learn into our own system.

Nothing happens without **motivation**. It is the engine of successful action. There is also etymological evidence of this close link. Motivation originates from the Latin *movere*, which means *moving*. Thus, it is about getting a process started, *to set* oneself in motion.

Motivation also contains the **motive**, the reason. We lend our actions purpose and structure, assign them a time limit, and define individual steps that combine into a purposeful process.

The motive in music is also inspiring. Here the motive is viewed as a seed from which something engaging forms that can lend "the theme a characteristic imprint."[62]

---

61   Güllich & Krüger (2013, pg. 278).
62   Ehlert (n. d.).

And another analogy also provides interesting insights: photography. It starts with the subject, which requires accurately weighing up the long shot and close-up, the correct aperture, the right background, light, and overall composition. When the subject is placed into a harmonious setting, it will captivate the viewer.

Being captivated by the subject is what we're after. It is precisely that which allows us to achieve something, to create something, to evolve, and to improve ourselves. The subject or motive generates motivation, and motivation allows us to embrace even unpleasant things.

Accepting effort, even when it hurts, is the level we should reach. However, why do it laboriously and arduously if there is a less laborious alternative? The effort is our trouble spot, the spot where, to use a medical analogy, a nerve is extremely sensitive to pressure. Building resilience against that moment is worth striving for, especially when your goals are ambitious.

Fortunately, I never had problems enduring major exertion. On the contrary, for me, physical effort is almost an addiction.

Nevertheless, there are moments that make us reflect and pose the question: why am I doing all of this? I had a lot of doubts during the preparation phase for the 2021 season. The pandemic had been very challenging. All those tournaments without spectators and without atmosphere, which, of course, also tested our motivation. It was time to reflect:

- *Where am I and where do I want to go?*
- *How many times do I want to endure this drudgery?*
- *How long do I want to keep playing?*
- *How long will my body be able to do this?*

One Friday afternoon, I had completed an extremely tough unit on the court, it was the final day of a very tough training week, and my body had to work really hard. So, when, after at least three hours, I slumped to the ground completely exhausted and gasping for air, I had a pivotal moment: I realized that I love this type of overexertion.

As absurd as it sounds, I get the most joy out of this grueling part of the work, and it is the reason why I continue to do it. To burn off energy, to push my physical and mental limits just a little more each time, to optimize details to get a little closer to my goals. I could not and cannot imagine living without all that.

The industry now entices those struggling with willpower with *outsmarting* themselves. Since many people struggle with getting motivated to go on even a regular little endurance run, the app industry, with its sophisticated technology, has been lending a hand. Clever app creators exploit this shortcoming and frequently develop very beneficial apps with their **activity trackers**.

The cognitive foundation has been laid. People know that they tend to not get enough exercise as the media is constantly reminding them. But they struggle to correct this state under their own steam. The effects of pertinent apps are tested on thousands of test subjects. A "small to moderate effect on physical activity behavior"[63] was detected, but no more than that. And so, it remains arduous.

There is no efficient way around it, we must start with ourselves, deep within ourselves. We are again looking at elite sports. That means staying perpetually motivated. On a grand scale, it means years of staying unceasingly enthusiastic about training and competing and summoning

---

63   Jablinski (2021, pg. 122)

the willpower to fight off the occasional lack of willingness. On a small scale, it means being able to direct and thereby control one's motivation, to access it when needed, even when it's freezing outside and there are no spectators.

Motives can vary greatly. They can be about showing performance, demonstrating power, or making connections.[64] Usually it is a mix of several motives of varying degrees. These, in turn, are linked to action, action result, and action success.

Hence, there is the possibility that the action alone provides the sole and sufficient stimulus, for instance, when the experience of hiking in the mountains is motivated by the desire to hike in the mountains. This ideal level of motivation does not require us to overcome something; we can simply be. Such moments are, of course, highly valuable. But when it comes to high-performance processes, it's not enough to limit oneself to these feel-good areas.

The purpose of our pursuit, even if it does inspire us, requires concessions. For example, those who choose not to drive a car for environmental reasons must often accept spending more time bridging distances, being dependent on public transportation, and carrying their bags instead of putting them in the trunk of the car. Or someone who wishes to shine with every detail of their presentation in the morning must work into the night, despite fatigue.

And anyone wishing to become an Olympic champion must complete training sessions that very often go way beyond the feel-good areas. It can be the strength-sapping last bench press repetition, overcoming cramping in the final moments of a competition, or fighting cold wind gusts in the supposedly always-a-good-mood sport of beach volleyball. Purely motivational approaches shifting toward volitional processes are part of the high-performance system. Being able to exceed limits becomes a basic quality.

---

64 Güllich & Krüger (2013, pg. 279f.).

The conditions at the French Open 2020 were miserable. Due to the Covid pandemic, the tournament had been moved from May to October. Once again, players and team members were only allowed to leave the hotel for training and matches. Our movement range was limited to our room and the tennis court.

We regularly played in temperatures below 10 degrees Celsius. The court was soaked from lots of rain showers and the wind was icy cold. Weather, courts, temperatures, no spectators due to the pandemic—nothing worked! There wasn't a hint of a Grand Slam atmosphere. It was dismal and demotivating. Additionally, I was dealing with massive back pain after a training session in the opening days.

When I once again came up against Kristina Mladenovic in the first match on the Court Philippe Chatrier, I quickly fell behind to 1:5. Everything felt unreal, unimportant, not relevant. All my actions felt like they should not happen that day.

I was disappointed in myself and especially in my feelings, and I had a guilty conscious because I had expected more professionalism, more inner motivation from myself. After all, we were at a Grand Slam tournament!

I thought that I might be overplayed and tired from the recent long weeks at the US Open 2020 in the United States. Sure, I had a Grand Slam win in doubles in the bag—an amazing experience! But that helped surprisingly little with my disappointment in singles at the US Open. I had recently suffered a decisive loss there in the first round, and that match left me with the bad aftertaste and the feeling that I would never make it to the second week of a Grand Slam in singles.

Here in Paris, I had no choice but to force myself to continue. Like a robot I worked for point after point, and I managed to turn the game around.

During the first set, I was able to defend six set points and ended up winning the match 7:5 and 6:3. Actually a good performance, but the lack of motivation and the aversion caused by the poor conditions would not go away.

What to do when I dislike something: push past the limits my body had clearly set with a vengeance. And I did so by only being able to play every match with the help of several painkillers. But I also knew that, as a pro athlete, one has to push oneself in certain situations, and a Grand Slam main draw on my favorite surface was such a situation.

And so, I dragged my spirit and my body from match to match. On the days off in-between, I drove to clinics for MRIs[65] of my back or made phone calls to specialists who could potentially help me in the short run. The tournament doctors were of no help, which was surprising and disappointing. They merely supplied me with an adequate amount of pain medications.

With every win I increasingly came to terms with the situation; I was never satisfied with my performance but always glad when, in the evenings, I could lay in bed with a heated pad against my back. With clenched teeth I defeated Martić, at that time ranked seventeenth in the world, in three sets.

The win on that gloomy afternoon when the floodlights had to be turned on already at 4 p.m., transported me to the second week of a Grand Slam tournament in singles for the first time in my career. Not very glamorously, but still a major milestone. I ultimately made it all the way to the quarter final.

Paris 2020 is an extreme example, but during my career, I have endured many situations that might have caused someone to give up. Often the most miserable conditions yielded the best results. But here only one recipe will work: refusing to give up!

---

65   Magnetic resonance imaging.

One thing is for sure, motivation determines the willingness to train and perform and sets the pace for our athletic behavior. Marion Sulprizio and Jens Kleinert of the German Sport University Cologne differentiate four **motivational problem situations**:

- First, beginning but not sticking it out,

- Secondly, **not wanting to,**

- Third, **sticking it out but not being any good**, and

- Fourth, **wanting to but not having the nerve to try.**[66]

Problem situation one, *beginning but not sticking with it*. Here we can see one of the basic mental intersections associated with the questions:

- How long will I keep up with my opponent's pace?

- How long do I dare to keep up?

- Give up or keep going?

- Push through the pain or choose a medical timeout?

The line between decisions is razor-thin and—this is the good news—can be moved. Sometimes the line moves toward the growing resilience that is barely perceptible in the background when we raise our overall performance level.

But sometimes it is our lack of motivation that gets in the way of an overall performance increase. And something else to consider is the impact of the **form of the day**, the opponent's demeanor, and the level of the athletic competition.

- So how much reserve do we have when we are confronted by the work, the task, or the moment?

66   Kleinert & Sulprizio (2019, pg. 173f.).

- How do we resist the temptation to just throw in the towel and get the immediate reward of rest and pleasant lack of purpose?

One important initial measure is not to let oneself get carried away by spontaneous thoughts but to think beyond the moment:

- How would I feel just moments after abandoning my activity?

- Would I be at peace with myself or furious that I was so weak-minded?

- How would it affect the goals I set?

Hence the name of the game is: anticipating delayed emotional consequences and doing a retrospective assessment.

Anticipating tomorrow's emotions

If we consider choosing to abandon our action, we must also consider first that the subsequent despair can long outlast the competition. That the feeling of lack of strength, endurance, and willpower will reverberate and affect subsequent training and tournament slots. Self-doubt can crop up, and the issue of the next problem situation will follow seamlessly and unwanted.

Not wanting to. This is certainly the exception in high-performance sports, because the strong commitment that elite sports demand also requires a minimum of desire and willingness to achieve. A lack of volition is more likely to occur during childhood when participating in sports can be more due to parents' ambition rather than a child's desire.

In an adult elite athlete, a lack of volition surfaces due to overtraining because, for instance, the athlete failed to balance long training and competition phases with adequate regenerative phases away from the sport.

And what about the motivational problem situation, *sticking it out* or *not being any good*?[67] Here we must first differentiate:

- Is it about limited individual potential?

- Or, is the potential not being tapped or are the wrong approaches being used?

The former should bring up the question of what is the aspiration with which I approach the activity, and is it beneficial even if I may never be convincing in this task. Weighing these options ideally leads to the decision to stay or to move on to other things.

But the case is very different if my poor performance is due to misdirected potential. That's when I have to analyze, readjust, and initiate new processes. Either way, this brings up the question of prognosis for the future.

- Which indicators provide me with information about if and how far I can make it?

- For instance, is **talent**—its accurate measurability is certainly debatable—a reliable aspect?

In California, 1,528 children with a high IQ were subjects in a long-term study. The children were tested again forty years later, and were divided into two groups: the successful group and the unsuccessful group. The goal was to learn more about the reason for success. It turned out that people who were already more ambitious, more active, and more persistent as children and also had more active hobbies, participated more in group activities as adults, and preferred to *participate* in sports rather than *watch*.[68] According to the attention-demanding result, discipline is a stronger predictor of success than talent.[69]

---

67 Kleinert & Sulprizio (2019, pg. 174).
68 Myers (2008, pg. 544), quote by Coleman (1980).
69 Ibidem.

It sounds less attention-demanding but at least as convincing and clear from Georg Hackl's mouth: "I may have a certain amount of talent. But what matters most is that you do what you do passionately and vigorously." And: "You simply can't ever give up!"[70]

Even as a child, I enjoyed working on a task until I mastered it. I particularly liked it when others had already given up. That has not changed even today; I've just reached a different level of physical and mental exertion. It's no longer a game.

But the seed was always there. Presumably it is a certain talent, a natural ability to endure exertion, in fact, to want to endure exertion. How the environment handles ambition and perseverance is almost certainly a factor. Will I be rewarded or derided?

When I was four years old, my parents, my brother, Arlen, and I moved to Saudi Arabia for three years. My father worked on developmental-aid projects as an engineer. I attended an English preschool and later first grade. My parents looked for a tennis coach for us and found a very good one: Tony Mmoh, the father of intermittently top-100 tennis player Michael Mmoh.

Several times a week, we traveled across Riyadh for training. Tennis and fitness training were combined. Mmoh had an uncanny talent for making ten children of various ages and different origins sweat, sometimes even until we dropped.

70   Brunner (2019, pg. 54).

As a six-year-old I would train there for three, four hours at a time with children four or five years older, like my brother. However, I was treated the same, and had to do the same exercises, without regard for my age.

And I—ambitious by nature—wanted to, of course, be just as good and learned early on to confront major challenges without complaining, without self-pity.

Such experiences fueled and reinforced my already present talent for persevering. My appetite for challenges and especially for physical exertion continues to be one of the greatest sources of joy and gratification.

And I was always certain that with outstanding discipline and daily hard work—harder than the others—I could not fail to reach my goals. If I wasn't ready to do anything for my goals, nothing would happen.

- Why do some people set high-performance standards while others are easily satisfied?

- Why do some people achieve more, are more successful, while others barely get ahead, or even fail?

Achievement motivation is a critical incentive. It involves striving for outstanding performances, the desire for control, and quickly reaching high standards paired with the hope for success and fear of failure.[71]

"Achievement motivation is the desire to achieve something important, to dominate things, people and ideas as well as keeping up high standards."[72] That is also the opinion of national coach Heiner Brand.

---

71   Myers (2008, pg. 544).
72   Ibidem (pg. 545.).

WILD CARD

"Even apparent genius has a source," he wrote in his book *Projekt Gold*, after leading his team to the 2007 World Champions title, "and most of the time it's hard work."[73]

That brings up the question of which types of motivation build a successful foundation. We are all familiar with the debate around **intrinsic** and **extrinsic motivation**.

- Is performance only possible if the desire originates within us, meaning it is initiated intrinsically?

- Or is success also possible with externally initiated control, discipline, and even reward?

When I began to play tennis, I was intrinsically motivated. I came from a tennis family; both my parents and my older brother liked to play and did so a lot in the evenings during the week and on the weekends. You might say it was our family sport.

That changed when I was a young adult, during the tough years on the small professional circuit— the ITF tournaments. In those days, when I had little money and had to live from hand to mouth to finance my tournaments, extrinsic motivation increasingly replaced intrinsic motivation. Tennis became my job.

It was about playing as well as possible and keeping my head above water so that later on I would be able to fulfill my big dream of making a good living from tennis.

Whether I enjoyed training, tournaments, or the nomadic life became secondary. I usually had to travel by myself since I couldn't afford a permanent trainer or fitness coach or physical therapist. Those were hard times that greatly shaped my type of motivation.

---

73   Brand & Löhr (2008, pg. 128).

A top performance can be inspired by a number of motives. It can be the desire for material betterment or, as previously mentioned, demonstrating performance and power, but also social recognition. Striving for fame, honor, sometimes for records, is ubiquitous in high-performance sports.

It is also why top players in their field, such as Martina Navratilova, will occasionally make a comeback, or players such as Roger Federer may try to break through the age-related, biological barriers.

Top performance as a general attitude

The desire for top performances does not have to be limited to sports. For instance, Bernhard Langer is a person who "always gives 100%. Everything I do I want to do well. Even if it's just sweeping the courtyard or cleaning my shoes."[74]

In hindsight I think that it is also possible to get very far with extrinsic motivation, in sports as well as in life. Whatever propels us, be it money, material possessions in general, prestige, fame, proving something to others, or all of the above—it can all be a powerful driver for top performances.

Yet I am deeply convinced that anyone who wants to fully and completely exploit their potential and feel gratification while doing so will also need to find a little joy in the thing itself. The feeling of doing something out of pure desire without thinking about the price money is indispensable.

If you want to bring out the best in yourself and feel truly satisfied, you can never let the fire that drove you in the beginning go out completely.

74   Brunner (2020, pg. 49).

WILD CARD

Drive and vision correlate.

- What do I plan to do?

- Today, this season, long term?

The degree of motivation primarily depends on who sets the goal.

- Do we work motivated by others or of our own volition?

The level of motivation gets shaky when the goal and the associated action is determined from the outside. For example, by ambitious parents who want their child to learn to play the violin without—and this is the critical point—the child having the desire to do so.

Extrinsic and intrinsic motivation blend if the parents are also musicians and the child recognizes the motive of continuing a family tradition. Violin lessons would be most effective for reaching the goal if the child is fascinated by the instrument and has frequently picked up the mother's violin and played air violin to imitate her. This results in maximum self-determination and motivation.

What applies to children also sets the tone in the adult world. Of course, as we get older, we might be more accepting of the idea that not everything we do in life brings us great joy. But that alone is not enough. Too many incomprehensible requirements by a superior over time are more likely to slow us down than inspire us.

Department heads, head coaches, and all other decision-makers should recognize this and provide objectives with a transparent motive. Or better yet, involve the other side in goal-setting. Or sometimes, even better than that, allow the other side to set their own goals.

The quality of motivation is determined by a nexus of very different influences.[75]

- What does our brain tell us?

- What do our emotions tell us?

- Which experiences do we look back on?

- How prevalent is a future outlook?

- What role do our conscious and subconscious minds play in this conflict situation?

It must be clear that the level of motivation can quickly change and even move in the opposite direction. An adult's motivation to participate in sports is significantly impacted by the exercise-related socialization of his youth.

Fifteen adults who gave exercise a wide berth took part in in-depth interviews. They were asked why they did not exercise,[76] "no time" was a frequently made argument.

The true reasons, particularly negative experiences with sports during childhood, emerged over the course of the conversation. Those in question were teased in PE class or pushed in the water at the pool. Parents, friends, PE teachers, classmates—all of them contributed to their sports-related socialization, often stifling the students' motivation for exercise.

GOALS PROPEL US

Once a year, we all become true World Champions in goal-setting, all on the same day. What a highly energetic moment. We promise to do this or that in the coming year.

---

75 Kleinert & Sulprizio (2019).
76 Brunner (1988).

WILD CARD

To stop smoking, eat less meat, to finally get more exercise. Statistics show that in 2021, approximately two-thirds of Germans made New Year's resolutions to reduce or avoid stress, spend more time with family and friends, do more for the environment, and get more exercise or participate in sports.[77]

These statistics are based on cross-sectional data. Results from a longitudinal study, meaning a one-year comparison, to see who reached their goals and who didn't, would be even more interesting. We could then see how clear intentions, and even those made in fun, potentially yielded one or two successes. Without a doubt the **motivation** to live a healthier life increases just by naming a specific **goal**.

When body and mind work in unison, we can take a crucial step toward our goals.

---

77   Statista Research Department (2022a).

A goal is motivation's greatest power source. Goals point the action in the right direction and fix our attention. We saw this with the Olympic gold medalist rower Michael Steinbach, and with Klay Thompson, the NBA's three-point recordholder. Their paths were determined by a clearly defined goal, which they were ultimately able to reach. "I am asking: where are my performance limits?", said Daniel Albrecht in the documentary *Streif*,[78] about the mystique of the worldwide notorious downhill ski course by the same name.

In the film, that statement was made by the top downhill ski racer after he overcame a terrible ordeal. In 2009, the Swiss skier had an accident on this downhill course in Kitzbühel. He crashed on the final jump at a speed of 138 kilometers per hour, flew 80 meters, and landed on his back and the back of his head. He was in a coma for three weeks, lost his memory and, month by month, fought to get his life back. In 2010, he made a comeback with the goal of figuring out the limits of his performance capacity.

Testing one's capabilities

These examples are impressive, not just because of the athletes' physical and mental strength but also due to the pull of the goals they set. It is therefore worth delving into this topic and extrapolating the consequences to actions.

We begin with day-to-day life. Setting general goals is not subject to a strategy. We do it continuously and intuitively. Goals inconspicuously guide us through life. They act in the background and provide a framework for our day-to-day actions.

We want to go from A to B, so we get on our bike or in the car and travel to the desired location. This latent linking and pursuing of goals shows how goals combine into a network that provides the necessary organization.

---

78   Streif—one hell of a ride (2015).

Scientists Müsseler and Rieger explain what is so special about goal-setting: "Goals change attention-, memory- and consciousness-related processes without the person intending to do so, and often without noticing these changes."[79] Even just the process of setting even nonspecific goals has effects.

When taking advantage of this basic cohesion and setting specific, ideally manageable goals, effectiveness is highly likely. To clarify, by contrast, for instance, in a game of chance, the result of which is not subject to personal influence. I may be motivated to win but am not included in the process. The decision of reaching the goal is not mine—t is completely coincidental.

Now we switch from day-to-day life to the performance category. Here, too, goals may be made independently without obvious mental control. But this is not about those goals. What matters here are the performance-oriented goals we set for our purposes to challenge ourselves, to focus, and to motivate.

Assigning a motive to actions

Beckmann and Elbe demonstrate the effect with an example from physical therapy. Patients with limited mobility in shoulders and elbows were asked to close their eyes and raise their arm as high as possible. The achieved performance could be increased by 18 degrees as soon as a specific instruction was added, such as taking a specific book off a shelf.[80]

Only when goals are firmly formulated are we able to measure ourselves against them. Ultimately, if the intended performance isn't previously anchored, anything can be declared a success. As the sports psychologist Hans Eberspächer adds so vividly, it would be like

79 Müsseler & Rieger (2017, pg. 242).
80 Beckmann & Elbe (2008, pg. 66).

shooting arrows at a wall and drawing the target around the arrows after hitting the wall.[81] That would be a recipe for self-deception.

As his colleague Lothar Linz, who has mentally stabilized multiple national teams, explains: "Wishes are much more likely to come true when they are unambiguously formulated. And we are much more likely to achieve goals when we have the courage to name them."[82]

Connecting with our goals

Formulating goals is not a succinct act. It's about content and choice of words. After all, all goals should have something binding, something the athlete can engage with and identify with. Important points include, among others, "the level of commitment to the goal" and the "confidence to be able to achieve it."[83]

But most of all it is about the aspiration that the goal reflects. How challenging and simultaneously realistic do I make my goal? We must start with a point of reference we can relate to.

So, before we define our desirable target state, we must focus on the actual state. Of course, the analysis must meet objective criteria otherwise legitimate goal-setting is inconceivable. Linz tells the athletes in his care: "Make your goal the best-possible result you can believe in."[84]

Goals are set based on the current performance level. They can apply to aspired-to results and rankings or to performance and actions. Multiple goals with multiple orientations are also possible.

---

81   Eberspächer (2012, pg. 32).
82   Linz (2014, pg. 82)
83   Müsseler & Rieger (2017, pg. 242)
84   Linz (2014, pg. 85).

When I was younger, I had specific goals in my head, always thought about a particular place in the rankings or particular results I wanted to reach. But I tend to be overambitious and, when I am focused on a goal, I cannot let it go; I get wound up in it.

Hence, I often suffered disappointments and my goals ended up putting more pressure on me than they benefited me.

But, of course, goals are important so we know where we want to go. And it's important to have intermediate goals so we can keep an eye on the structure.

- *Am I on the right path?*
- *Am I taking the right turn?*
- *Am I on schedule?*

But we should not just think about our goals and constantly ask ourselves how much further we have to go. Because that can drain us and wear us down, particularly during barren spells when things are moving slower than expected, such as phases during the tournament season with multiple early eliminations.

Outcome goals can be easily measured—we're either first or we're not—and can motivate long term. This is due to their superior nature. Winning gold at the Olympics or winning the Champions League are goals that must be set early and, therefore, must remain an irrevocable incentive over a long period of time.

Someone who sets an outcome goal—for instance, a ranking, a shooting percentage, a running time—sets a goal that is clearly measurable, which is an advantage later when verifying the result. At the same time, this focus on the outcome brings with it the risk of quickly and clearly sensing possible failure, which, depending on predisposition, can provoke fear of failure.

The fact that we don't have independent control over the result must also be taken into account. External influence on the result from, for instance, the trainer, opponent, or the weather is extensive. This factor must be considered when potentially failing to reach our goals.

But at the same time, we have to understand that we cannot always win and that losing is a natural, unavoidable part of athletic development. Sports psychologist Linz refers to Reinhold Messner[85], the first person to climb all eight-thousanders. But he, too, cannot claim a win. He made thirty expeditions into the superlative mountains but only managed to summit during eighteen of them.

- Did he fail twelve times?

- Or did he achieve his objective eighteen times?

Every goal category has its strengths. **Action-oriented goals** and achieving them depend primarily on oneself; a major advantage when causal relationships must be established. It is fundamental.

Because if I fail to meet my objective, or really overshoot the mark, I know where to find the causes: myself. That's honest, clear, and very direct, and it is a good basis for adjusting my goals if necessary. Because that, too, is a part of goal-setting: allowing myself to take stock.

Action-oriented goals stand the test across all sports. A study by Kieran M. Kingston and Lew Hardy[86] back in the 1990s showed that focusing on one's own actions is more effective than focusing on the result. With respect to golf, this means: "I will play the ball to the left of the tree onto the apron," instead of: "Today I will play a sixty-nine!" The authors argue for the effectiveness of **process-oriented goals**, especially when the complexity of a task must be reduced. This results in increased self-efficacy, which, of course, is near and dear to an ambitious performer's heart.

---

85   Linz (2014, pg. 83).
86   Kingston & Hardy (1997, pg. 289).

Particularly after my hiatus, I learned that a process-oriented perspective is much more helpful to me because I am better able to stay in the moment. And someone who is in the now is more efficient.

I therefore focused increasingly on manageable subgoals on my path, such as finding joy in training, valuing small improvements, and not merely defining myself by, for example, a good performance in a tournament.

Growing together with my team and viewing my development as a player and person as an ongoing task became increasingly important to me.

When asking people about the reason for their outstanding performance, the answer is often: "I simply focused on the next step," or: "I just played point by point."

These explanations show that often it's not about the distant goal but about the immediate and the next little step. And when we string these little steps together, in the end we're surprised at how far we've come. So, it's important to focus on the process, on negotiating the path to the goal.

I assess my process-oriented goals during the off-season period during the winter:

- *What is important to me for the new season?*
- *What do I want on and off the court?*
- *What do I want to maintain in my work and what do I want to optimize?*
- *Where do I see potential in my game and which improvements must be implemented to fully exploit this potential?*
- *How do we implement these improvements?*

Goals should be binding guidelines, but they should not be viewed as rigid benchmarks separate from accompanying circumstances. It is therefore wise to, from the start, set a date to take stock.

For example, someone with an unexpectedly good start of the season or World Cup could quickly pass his expectations. He could hardly expect motivational boosts from goals that are no longer adequate.

On the flipside: I am falling short of my performance. The reasons don't have to be due to inherent performance problems necessarily. Unexpected stress with a partner, simultaneous work stress, a move, an injury, flu, the pandemic, change of coach—there are many possible reasons that could not be anticipated beforehand.

We're better off if we can define our goal more broadly, like Bernhard Langer: "My main goal is to get better."[87]

Goals can also originate from the joint vision of entire teams, departments, classes, or other groups because certain results and rankings can only be achieved together as a team. Or they might arise because the team wishes to focus on a specific type of communication, training position, or playing attitude.

Together the group agrees on a list of objectives and makes it official by having everyone sign it as a voluntary commitment. And once the ink is dry, the agreement's proclaimed content must become an unconditional pledge that can extend to private life outside the stadiums and courts, athletic centers, and office buildings.

Because goals tend to be accompanied by compromises such as, for instance, loss of leisure time, I must consciously and decisively commit to sacrificing some of my freedom and autonomy. The goals agreement isn't binding in a legal sense, but it is very much so mentally.

---

87   Brunner (2020, pg. 50).

Fed-Cup 2017: That special feeling of a team success. Left to right: Barbara Rittner, Julia Görges, Angelique Kerber, Carina Witthöft, Laura Siegemund.

The question of how much influence an athletic goal should have on non-athletic, private life comes to the forefront time and again when teams are trying to advance. There tends to be a distinct transition when moving from the third to the second division, with the exception of soccer.

Away games, which previously had been limited to the region, are now often in other parts of the country. Game days suddenly consume the entire weekend. And training frequency has to increase to Sigmund keep up at that level. Instead of three days, players now train four or five days a week.

Regardless of the club's position and its financial resources, developing a common position is important to team cohesion. Two opposing camps would do significant damage to the working atmosphere and should be quickly moderated into a united team.

A THOUSAND HOURS OF DILIGENCE

Malcolm Gladwell refers to studies conducted with violin students at an elite academy in Berlin. All of them began at age five with two to three practice hours per week. At age eight, there were three groups with different practice levels.

The test results of the 20-year-old students found that those who had what it takes to become elite violinists could look back on an incredible 10,000 practice hours, the mediocre students had only 8,000 hours practice, and those studying to become music teachers only had 4,000 hours.

The psychologist K. Anders Ericsson, who conducted these studies, also studied amateur and professional pianists and got the same result. The professional musicians could claim 10,000 piano practice hours. His conclusion: "The people at the top don't just work harder or even much harder than everyone else. They work much, *much* harder."[88]

Those who wish to succeed would do well to train much, much harder than everyone else. Referencing neuroscientist Daniel Lezithin, Gladwell asserts this would result in a world-class performance in any line of work.

He also refers to the psychologist Michael Howe and his findings on the development of Wolfgang Amadeus Mozart, who did not consider the exceptional composer's early works as outstanding. Mozart also did not always play his own works.

---

88   Gladwell (2009, pg. 43).

Howe considers the piano concerto No. 9 K-271 to be the first authentic masterpiece, at which point Mozart had been a composer for ten years. "Ten-thousand hours is the magic number of greatness," says Gladwell.[89]

True success never happens overnight, even when it sometimes looks that way from the outside, but rather with continuity and tenacity. Focus, diligence, and discipline, not just short term but over a long period of time. Behind the success, there are always years of preparation, but sometimes those go completely unnoticed.

An unusual amount of tenacity is crucial in everyday training, which can be quite monotonous. Therefore, a common problem is coping with the "always the same." **Monotony** is motivation's acrimonious adversary.

Handling monotony creatively

How does a swimmer get in the pool over and over again and ambitiously swim kilometer-long training sessions while watching nothing but tiles pass by below, several hours a day, several days a week?

World-class swimmer Britta Steffen said in a 2019 interview that she personifies the water and talks to it.[90] Exchanging thoughts instead of not thinking. Swimming doesn't have to be so lonely. Depending on the individual, this idea can possibly be applied to other individual sports.

---

89 Ibidem (pg. 45).
90 Catuogno (2019).

I can't stand monotony. But the fact is that we cannot continue to reinvent the wheel, can't always pep up every little training session. Some elements of training are simply monotonous, but we still have to do them, in tennis as well as any other high-performance area.

You cannot avoid doing thousands upon thousands of repetitions if you want to continue to improve at the highest level. When I practice shots over and over again, repeat tiny changes in technique again and again with hundreds of shots, then—and this is my positive take on it—there is also something meditative about that. It is a mixture of ambition, flow, and the urge to optimize, maybe even optimization mania.

To be among the best at the top level, you need to be a little crazy. That is also apparent in those moments of unending monotony: doing something over and over again because you are obsessed with doing it just a little bit better than it already is. Because you see the potential and are still hanging on when others are already in the shower.

I believe in not only enduring the necessary monotony but also recognizing it as a part of the big picture, and therefore learning to enjoy it just a little. That's what sets the best apart.

Monotony cannot really be taken out of the training process, and is even intrinsic to some sports. For instance, endurance sports are characterized by repetition of the same movement patterns. It's no different in running than it is in swimming, or in rowing as it is in cycling.

So, monotony cannot be trivialized or even argued away. In spite of its negative connotation, it is not a curse for everyone or all the time. And those who find the monotony annoying should immediately do something about it.

It is obvious that any type of hard work becomes arduous at some point. It doesn't matter if it is a surgeon performing twenty-five surgeries in one day or me on the court trying to play a more precise forehand for the thousandth time. On our way to success, we always exceed the limits of what is strictly fun. It's part of wanting to set yourself apart from others.

That makes it all the more important to put a check on monotony as much as possible and, when things become laborious, make them as pleasant as is feasible within the given framework. There should be some balance between the sacrifices we have to make and the joy we find in the process on the way to achieving our goals.

When that balance is too unequal too often, we can no longer enjoy the challenge; the endeavor will drain us long term and we will be unable to bring our best possible performance.

Some initial suggestions come from **recreational sports**. The passionate runner notes the meditative character of running as his motivational stimulus. The swimmer refers to the overall proprioception after swimming 1,500 meters in the pool or a thirty-minute lap in a lake. So, it is possible to try and find new ways to access one's sport, which should be seen as an expansion rather than a substitution.

Let's take meditation, for instance. The circumnavigator Boris Herrmann said that for his next *Vendeé Globe* he would need to prepare better for the loneliness.[91] He therefore planned to learn about Buddhism and try to tap even more of his potential on this new path. Those who set their

---

91   ZDF-Sportstudio report (2022).

goals high must therefore extend their scope, allow for a wider perspective, and try something new. It improves preparation and increases motivation.

Back to general high-performance monotony: to tennis and badminton with the same training shots over and over again, to athletic training or boxing with their high number of repetitions, to shooting or competitive bowling with continuous focus on the same target, or top-golfers:

- How does a golfer, whose training only partially consists of aiming at holes and much more of stoically hitting balls on the driving range, manage to stay in a good mood during training?

This is especially difficult when, as a child or adolescent with very little self-discipline, one is not able to escape this very common performance methodology due to their talent and squad affiliation. Only one thing helps: "You have to love golf," says Arne Dickel, who was once on the Junior Ryder Cup team with Sergio García, was awarded Germany's Youth Trainer of the Year in 2019, and today coaches the First League club Munich GC. "The feeling of hitting the ball, feeling the contact, and the feeling of increasingly getting better at controlling the ball, compare to few other things in life."

So, monotony doesn't even arise when love of the sport supersedes it. Aside from that, variety helps to break up the monotony intrinsic to certain sports, at least briefly but effectively. Perhaps by inserting a short playing session into the long training session on the driving range: different stroke, different setting.

That interruption is necessary because "particularly on the driving range where golfers typically practice long shots, I frequently lose that lightness and thus the joy of playing," explains Pablo Brunner. The nineteen-year-old is a national league player and the training volume is high.

"That's when I really benefit from an hour of short shots. I can build in some playfulness and try out unusual things. For instance, how to produce maximum spin. Or how to play the ball really shallow or flag high." But all of this isn't just a way to add diversion but is also very important training as it increases the shot repertoire.

And when the movement during small-space putting gets lost in endless repetitions? "When I notice that I imagine with every putt lots of spectators watching at the final and decisive hole in a tournament. On the one hand, this helps me to immerse myself in my own little bubble, and on the other hand, it prepares the actual situation prior to that one important point in the next tournament. That moment will no longer feel unfamiliar."

It is important to pull out all the stops. As training age and quality of movement increase, leaps in performance get smaller. If a professional golfer wants to play one shot better in a tournament with four rounds, mathematically that would be a quarter shot per round. Such a homeopathic performance increase isn't even visible from the outside and barely perceptible for the golfer. But he must strive for it, make it his goal. That half a shot must motivate for a thousand hours of diligence.

Bernhard Langer's success was also preceded by a huge amount of endurance on the golf course. "I was there nearly every afternoon, definitely on weekends, all day during vacation, and sometimes we even pitched tents at the golf course. I was on the golf course when the sun came up. I stayed until the sun went down."[92]

THE ENJOYMENT FACTOR

Seven one-hundredths too slow, fourth place. Tears of disappointment instead of tears of joy. After the first Olympic slalom run in 2022, Lena Dürr was still in first place with 0.72 seconds ahead of Petra Vlhová, who ended up winning the race. Seven one-hundredths—too short to even call it a timespan, but long enough for permanent disappointment. At least it feels like one will be eternally sad.

---

92 Brunner (2020, pg. 47).

Emotions raise us up to levels of happiness or plunge us down into the depths of despair. And sometimes there are only seven one-hundredths of a second between both.

And yet it is this unpredictability that adds so much excitement. Since the outcome of an athletic competition is unknown at the start, we don't know who will throw up their hands jubilantly at the end. It is precipitated by the script—never established beforehand—that is written by the sport in real time. Emotional psychology is accompanied by physical symptoms, such as a change in heartbeat, breathing frequency, and overall body position.

Not only is the athlete overcome by emotion, but also the coaching staff, family, and friends. Michael Rösch, Olympic biathlon champion in 2006 and *Eurosport* television expert, held his goose-pimpled arm in front of the camera when Denise Herrmann won gold on February 7, 2022, in the fifteen-kilometer sprint in Peking two days before Lena Dürr just missed the podium. **Luck** and **frustration** live close together. That makes it tricky and necessitates in-depth engagement with one's emotions.

Below we will first focus on the positive emotions, and not just those we experience when we leave the ring as winners. This moment of distinct joy should simply be enjoyed; no need for a detailed analysis. It is much more interesting to take a look at our physical and mental state on the way to our goal.

When the anticipation is to win today, and the objective is to score a goal today, everything will simply focus on the completion of the action but not the processes that get us there. Thus, the athlete would subscribe to the notion that satisfaction can only be achieved by scoring that final goal. Conversely this means that the previous, and most likely very clever, play barely mattered, meaning it would be less important.

- Do we want that?

- Do we really want to limit the feeling of happiness to that brief moment of successful execution?

Appreciating the details

That would also put the painter's creative process in question—his initial sketches, those first brush strokes, layering the paint. Painters like Flemish artist Jan van Eyck added more than 100 layers of paint to their works. Is all of that meant to be just an emotionless means to an end?

Pure or even simple **anticipation** happens when we can take pleasure in the entire action. In ball sports that would be the underlying tactic, the initial pass, the feint, the dynamic dribbling of the ball toward the goal, the precise cross and then, but only then, possibly a successful finish.

In a work-related context it might be the pitch with which I want my agency to prevail over other agencies. Pure anticipation before the comparison showdown on day X is what all participants need to get to work with maximum efficiency and motivation. Enjoying the tinkering, the creative brainstorming, and developing strategies. It applies to all areas of life, from launching a startup all the way to coalition negotiations.

There are also analogies within the context of training.

Is the training the journey and the competition the destination? Both require **motivation** and both require **passion**. Is the build-up to an attack in handball or the approach to a jump shot only a means to an end of the joy of a potential goal, or are they themselves dignitaries of joyful processes? If they are not, we should immediately think about how we can promote them to the latter. Because it is always about valuing the whole. Here the basic (re)-structuring of one's personal philosophy is much more helpful than individual mental tools.

The more we are able to enjoy the challenge itself as well as all of its little interim stages, to value them, and view them as an opportunity for personal growth regardless of their success, the more successful we are in mastering them. And the further we ultimately get in the overall process.

We have reached a higher level of consciousness when all of this is no longer only theoretical and no longer perceived experience, but internalized action. Ultimately it is about automating everything to the point that it disappears from our consciousness.

"Man is a thinking being, but his great works are created when he isn't computing or thinking."[93] That is how Daisetsu Suzuki, the well-known Japanese author and professor of Buddhist philosophy during the 1920s in Kyoto, put it. He argues for the art of forgetting yourself. That is the focus of Buddhism-motivated archery.

This interpretation of archery also requires the archer to engage with himself. And that brings us back to our critical point, which is to not only (potentially not at all) define the action by its result.

In 1924, the philosopher Eugen Herrigel, who was very interested in mystical knowledge, followed the call to the university in Sendai, Japan. A propitious convergence of coincidences allowed him to take archery lessons from the famous Master Awa Kenzo.

---

93   Herrigel (2011), pg. 7

Awa's insights made Herrigel the pioneer of the **Zen-Buddhist** outlook on life in the West and resulted in the world-renowned book *Zen in the Art of Archery.*

Now, asking ourselves to internalize Zen Buddhism would be too much. Rather, we should focus on recognizing an important source of inspiration and harnessing it. For the newbie from Germany, concentrating solely on stretching the bow was a major effort and tested his patience to the point where he nearly lost it had it not been for the master, who demonstrated how relaxed his own arms were as he stretched the bow. And he also explained to his student, Herrigel, that he wasn't breathing properly.

The breath as a source of strength

It is recommended that after inhalation, the **breath** be pushed down gently until the abdominal wall feels slightly taut. The breath should then be held there for a while and finally released, slowly and evenly. According to Master Awa Kenzo, this way of breathing will allow us to discover the source of all mental strength.

Well? Did it help with archery? Our Western impatience demands to know. It did! The necessary effort continuously decreased.[94]

Without going into further detail here about this technique, some things are becoming clear: patience is a factor, as well as openness to a yet unfamiliar approach; also separating action from result, believing in the power of the breath, and finally, not thinking, but letting it happen.

In the spirit of the autogenic formula for breathing: my breathing is very calm; it breathes me.

That is not just the perspective of Buddhism-inspired Eugen Herrigel, but also that of the well-known sports educator Timothy Gallwey.

---

94 Ibidem.

"Few great shots are played when the mind is fixed on the position of the feet, the behavior of the left arm, etc." he warned all golfers who think too much during their shots.[95] Instead, he recommends a relaxed type of concentration: "Relaxed concentration is the key to excellence in all things."[96]

It is important to train our inner abilities, to be aware, to choose an action and have **faith** in the decision: "awareness, choice, and trust."[97] And that mind shift can potentially reach even further and grasp our general view of our own performance process.

One insight helped me lot on my own journey. It is obvious, yet I did not truly understand it for many years on the tennis circuit.

Not just myself, but also the other players try to set themselves apart from the competition. They, too, make sacrifices to ultimately be the winner. Until I had that insight, I had viewed my opponents as a kind of necessary evil, a kind of object in a game that was meant for me, and that I wanted to win.

Then I realized that some of them came from far worse circumstances than I and had a rockier road than mine to get to where they are now.

This insight helped me enormously to value my own work, to be grateful for my very own journey, and for being one of the players on this tennis circuit.

---

95   Gallwey (2015).
96   Ibidem (pg. 17).
97   Ibidem (pg. 16).

Sometimes we catch ourselves feeling jealous toward the competition when they are doing better than we are. Surely that's human. But I try to figure out where that feeling is coming from. Because, ultimately, it makes no sense to be jealous. Jealousy inhibits our own actions.

- *Am I disappointed because I haven't gotten as far?*
- *Is it based on self-doubt that I won't be able to perform similarly well?*
- *Or does it hurt my pride if I don't perform as well; am I just a sore loser?*

Having the courage to see behind our own curtain to learn the true reasons for our feelings moves us forward.

What matters is appreciation and gratitude for our own game and, more broadly, for our own athletic existence. This can result in profound inner satisfaction, happiness.

The psychologist Csikszentmihalyi accuses man of not knowing how to live happiness. He refers to Aristotle who, all the way back in antiquity, assumed that man seeks happiness.[98] But man has not learned to make happiness the absolute purpose in life. Csikszentmihalyi makes it clear that health, beauty, money, and power are not equivalent to happiness.

He explains that "happiness isn't something that just happens. It is not the consequence of pleasant coincidences. It isn't anything that can be bought with money or appropriated with power. It does not depend on external events, but rather on how we interpret them. Happiness is a state for which one has to be ready, which every individual must cultivate and defend."[99]

---

98   Csikszentmihalyi (2017, pg. 15).
99   Ibidem. (2017, pg. 16).

© picture alliance, Marijan Murat, dpa

Enjoying the moment: Opening the heart after winning the semi-final against the world's number two in 2016.

Csikszentmihalyi was the director of the "Quality of Life Centers" and Professor of Business Management at Claremont Graduate University in California. He is considered one of the first to delve into the **flow** state. His basic theory refers to a "state in which one is so focused on an activity that nothing else seems to matter."[100] The psychologist Renate Frank refers to a state of absorption and complete concentration and "someone being in the zone, completely and totally oblivious to his surroundings."[101]

---

100   Csikszentmihalyi (2017, pg. 19).
101   Frank (2008, pg. 92).

123

Scientific findings and literary contributions show that the dimension of flow must be split. While one raises the flow to a level of an exhilarating runner's high, the feeling for the other already begins when various physical-emotional processes are in sync with each other. Eberspächer refers to Mihaly Csikszentmihalyi[102] and summarizes the components of a flow experience as follows:

- *Ability and demand requirement. The individual feels optimally engrossed, and in spite of high demand has the sure feeling of still being in control of the action.*

- *Action requirements and feedback are experienced as clear and free of interpretation, so the individual knows what to do at all times and without having to think about it.*

- *The action flow is experienced as smooth. One step fluidly transitions to the next as if the action were gliding from an internal logic. (The term "flow" likely originated from this component.)*

- *The individual does not have to deliberately concentrate, rather concentration happens by itself, similar to breathing. Any cognition that does not have an immediate bearing on regulating the current execution is blocked.*

- *The way time is experienced is greatly affected. The individual loses a sense of time and doesn't know how long he has been engaged in the activity. Hours pass like minutes.*

- *The individual no longer experiences himself separate from the activity, but rather loses himself completely in his activity ("merging" of self and activity).*

Eberspächer (2011, pg. 31).

---

102   Csikszentmihalyi (1975).

When someone experiences flow in tennis, he no longer thinks about things like wanting to win, beating this particular opponent, or what the consequences of winning or losing might be. You might say the player has moved beyond the level of thinking.

The game has gotten much bigger than the final result. You experience a kind of exhilaration during which it's only about the way in which you master the game overall.

When asking a player about his flow experience, about what he thought about during the match, you will get answers like: "I simply concentrated on the next point, let go of everything else, just played, shot for shot."

Letting go, getting into it, losing sight of the goal for a while, and instead becoming one with the path to the goal—all of that is characteristic of the flow and the moments in which we bring our best performances.

"It's about something fluid, weightless, during which happiness appears completely unintentionally,"[103] adds Renate Frank, doctor of psychology at the University of Giessen. Frank, head of postgraduate psychotherapist training, hereby describes general, pleasurable happiness. It is not just about pure stimulation of sensory input. A state of flow requires a challenging effort determined by a degree of difficulty that can only just be managed. According to Frank, profound gratification and even gratitude appear as a reward for the successful task accomplishment. "This is sometimes perceived as a blessing."

As children we become familiar with the beginnings of this feeling without knowing that we just entered the science-based flow tunnel. For instance, when the parents don't drive up to the castle at the top of a hill but park in the valley to conquer the hill and castle with their children on

---

103   Frank (2008, pg. 92f.).

foot, the feeling at the entrance to the castle is then completely different. A mixture of pride and authenticity, almost like they have a lunch date with the king and queen. It is similar to the skier who doesn't take the gondola to the top, but conquers the elevation gain under his own steam by skinning up. Even the view will feel different and not just for miles but beyond the horizon.

Athletic activity is verifiably beneficial to the quantitative and qualitative feeling of happiness. As part of a meta study, Petra Jansen and Sabine Hoja conducted eight studies to see what they would reveal about sports as a happiness facilitator. Six of these studies provided scientific evidence that athletic interventions have a positive effect on our sense of happiness.[104]

It therefore makes sense that sports science has long attended to the subject. The researchers point out that the flow experience was already addressed in the 1930s as part of the theory of Gestaltkreis, and defines flow as an "emotional state that results from completely losing oneself in an activity and arises from the joy in executing the same. The process is experienced as a consistent flowing from one moment to the next. This results in a kind of centering of the attentiveness that causes the activity itself to become the purpose and goal of the action."[105]

As Eberspächer writes, it leads to a concentrated narrowing as soon as the individual enters the state of flow. "The individual experiences himself very vividly as he performs a movement sequence. For instance, a butterfly swimmer imagines he is 'flying' or a ballroom dancer imagines he is 'floating.'"[106]

This creates a very rhythmic and vivid image that becomes the basis for a solid, situation-appropriate movement implementation. The happiness hormones gladly receive these emotions and put the body on track. Emotions become perceptions and those, in turn, generate meaning.[107]

---

104   Jansen & Hoja (2018).
105   Röthig & Prohl (2003, pg. 201).
106   Eberspächer (2012, pg. 82).
107   Myers (2008, pg. 258 et seq.).

SUMMARY

Goals are essential guides to mastering first steps. But during the process, it is advisable to focus frequently on the conscious perception of one's small developmental steps and moments with positive actions in particular.

UNDERSTANDING THE CONTEST
Satisfaction should not only result from winning *** refrain from black-and-white thinking *** invest your energy in the things you can control *** nurture your autonomy *** develop a belief in self-efficacy *** engage in your personal development process.

THE POWER OF MOTIVATION
Visions as motivators *** set (verifiable) goals for yourself *** provide situational incentives *** accept effort *** discipline is often more powerful than talent *** take into account the form of the day *** emotion, reason, mindset, and experience affect motivation.

GOALS HELP YOU GET A MOVE ON
The pulling effect of goals *** goals change attention, memory, and awareness processes *** nail down directives *** choose goals that are both challenging and realistic *** results, rankings, performances, actions, and emotions can become goals *** goals are binding.

ONE-THOUSAND HOURS OF DILIGENCE
Top athletes have more training hours *** accept monotony instead of enduring it *** overcome monotony, for instance, with a meditative perspective *** allow for creativity to lessen monotony.

THE ENJOYMENT FACTOR
Develop joy in the process *** finding yourself *** happiness as a state one has to be ready for *** flow as a reward.

© picture alliance, Julian Stratenschulte, dpa

3

Overcoming
a point deficit

LOST SET: TURNING CRISES INTO OPORTUNITIES

The point deficit is an everyday phenomenon. It is an obtrusive companion that constantly reminds us how much we still have to get done. "You're behind," he cynically whispers in our ear. At first, we ignore him and shake off his commentary. After all, we hope to get back into the game. Until the creep speaks up again: "You're still behind, now even more so."

The deficit is a vicious fellow who manages to turn our positive thinking incrementally into negative emotions. And the further our performance lags behind our original objective, the more the negative takes root and spreads inside us. After getting into our head, it then starts on our body, energy decreases, and thereby our performance.

At some point we fall so far behind our former aspirations that we can hardly see ourselves being able to cope with all that we have missed on and put off everything we need to do to catch up. Now, for the final showdown, the issue is in our head: fear arises. The belief that we are able to get ourselves out of a difficult situation by our own efforts is gone.

In day-to-day life it helps to shift priorities. Deficits melt away. We can scale back a little *here*, save a little time *there*, and deliberately reposition ourselves. But it's not that easy in performance sports. There we cannot escape the immediate confrontation.

The here and now requires immediate problem-solving; there is no time to contemplate priorities. A new and eager title aspirant lies in wait. Winning is the top priority, that is sport's logic. Failing is not an option.

"Brass" has become the derogatory term for the fictitious medal material of the fourth-place Olympian. Unfortunately, it doesn't count that I left countless athletes behind just by qualifying and traveling to the Olympics. And it also doesn't matter that I beat many world-class athletes to a fourth-place finish. All that matters is the win.

Thus, we must develop action alternatives that we can quickly and uncompromisingly prioritize ahead of anything adverse and implement.

How do we rise above the point deficits in life? We can simply refuse to acknowledge a deficit as such—sometimes we don't recognize the most ordinary tools. A point deficit only has power over us to the extent that we choose to see it as a powerful opponent.

Minimizing the threat

An occasionally successful approach is to poke fun at a threat with a little hubris. The threat loses its power when we turn it into ridicule. It diminishes, and at that moment when it is at its most vulnerable, we strike and dismantle it.

Our opponent's body language can be overwhelmingly self-confident. But it could also be an act ready for the stage. Or a satirical distortion of an average person. Or a disguised operative, an avatar, our own mirror image.

These examples may seem a bit bizarre, but they are meant to illustrate how this kind of over-exaggeration can allow us a brief inner chuckle. Sometimes, that brief moment is enough to trigger a change. Here creativity would be a helpful tool.

A totally different option: We can try to accept the point deficit. It happens, and it will most likely pass. We are familiar with this form of acceptance from the introductory words of various relaxation techniques: "sounds come and go" to prevent sudden noises from feeling intrusive. Instead, they should be accepted as natural companions.

We can develop a similar approach to our emotions. They come and, depending on how much power we give them in their interactions with us, they also go. If we give *them* the right to exist, we allow *ourselves* the option to let them move on, possibly to even incorporate them in a meaningful way before they disappear as a small lesson from which we may emerge invigorated.

In our world, and especially in an athletic competition, the unexpected—as well as the unwelcome—lurks everywhere. Anyone who doesn't have a plan is unlikely to leave the court a winner.

Rarely does everything work out 100 percent, neither in preparation nor in the match itself. What looks elegant and easy from the outside is active, precisely controlled tuning on the inside.

Bringing the activation level to an optimal point and keeping it there, working to play close to one's ideal level, starting with the first ball—this process depends on many factors. Implementing a tactic exactly as it was discussed beforehand with the coach isn't always successful. But what to do when it doesn't go as expected?

It's important to block out negative aspects and to accept external adversities as part of the game: the food that now inexplicably feels heavy in my stomach even though I was careful to eat the right things. That must be accepted just like any other physical complaints. The tightness in the calf that I already felt a few days ago and thought it had passed. Suddenly it's back, but it can't matter. The spectator in the yellow jacket sitting right where the opponent's ball toss hangs in the air and makes the ball all but disappear—it must not affect me. After all, I can't tell the spectator to sit somewhere else or take off his jacket.

Or technical elements from the game: the slice serve that worked great an hour before during practice, is suddenly gone. And it was the primary component of my tactics . . .

We need action strategies so we don't lose control. Mental (finessing) techniques should be as important in a sport as practicing shooting, hitting, and throwing techniques. So how do we proceed when we are at risk of losing control over the action?

These days, it is not unusual for scores in doubles to be somewhat random. This is due to the no-add counting method that was changed a few years ago. That means with a 40:40 score, the next point decides the match. And it is also due to the match tiebreak, a long tiebreak of up to ten points instead of a third set.

There were times when my partner Vera Zvonareva and I were behind 1:4 in a match because we lost two add-on points. It could just as well have been 3:2 in our favor. A mere two points made the difference in a three-game deficit, which may have also unfortunately gone against us.

In cases like this it is important to just ignore the deficit and to tell yourself: "We're playing well. It's an even match, the score is completely misleading. We must not change our strategy."

OVERCOMING ADVERSITY

The US philosopher Reinhold Niebuhr's greatly overused serenity prayer offers this helpful suggestion: "Grant me the serenity to accept the things I cannot change, courage to change the things I can, and wisdom to know the difference."[108]

---

108 This quote is attributed to Reinhold Niebuhr (1892–1971), US theologian and philosopher.

I can't really do anything about my tight calf; if anything, I should have addressed it before the match, but now I have to accept it. However, I should be alarmed by the repeatedly botched serve, and I should feel required to bravely counter it. Again and again, I am confronted with situations to which I must react and that require me to make a decision. But, incorporating Niebuhr's recommended division, the decision-making can be reduced to simple questions:

- Change?

- Or accept?

That might be reminiscent of the coincidence-guided plucking of flower petals by new lovers, but is indeed a decision-making process that results from practice and experience and consequent intuition. But the pressure situation in a competition under the pressure of time forces a masterful player to view his situation from the outside and to draw the appropriate conclusions wisely.

Sometimes, when I don't have a good start to a match, I wish I could press a button and rewind to the start. I tell myself, "I would do it better." Such nonsense! You either bring it on the court when it matters or you can pack up and go home. It is ruthless.

But that is precisely what makes it so special: knowing that you don't get a second chance. That it has to work right now, somehow, with every ounce of will, with all your strength—and with lots of resilience. Accepting that and loving the game in its entirety, with all its uncertainty, that is true strength.

Worried about an upcoming tennis match? That's part of it, writes Jeff Greenwald in his book *The best tennis of your life*.[109] But someone who wants to play the best tennis of their life must classify worries in good due time before they turn into anxiety. According to Greenwald, it is important to differentiate between productive and unproductive worrying.

Manageable and unmanageable worries

Productive worries relate to circumstances that are within our control and that drive us to do all we can for a best possible performance. These would include, for instance, restringing the rackets in good time, putting essential items in the tennis bag, or organizing a court and a partner for the warm-up.

By contrast, **unproductive worries** are outside of our control: thoughts about whether we will win or lose the game. Or what effect the result would have on our world ranking. Or what other people would think of me if I lose.

That's why we need to ask ourselves in the moment if we can change something. No? Then let go of the worries. Yes? Then, as per Greenwald: *"find time to make a list of things you can do, step-by-step, to productively work towards your goals."*[110]

When we are able to acquire this resilience in dealing with adversity, it is important that we become aware of this worthy ability. It boosts our self-confidence. And that results in feedback. Self-confidence and resilience, they play the ball back and forth; they grow hand in hand.

---

109   Greenwald (2007, pg. 10f.)
110   Ibidem. (pg. 12).

One prominent example of how I must handle adversity stems from the first round match at the Mutua Madrid Open in 2017, against Johanna Konta. I was ranked number thirty-five on the world ranking list, Konta was number seven. That day we were scheduled as the fifth match, and were supposed to take the court after the men's match, which can take forever when there are five sets.

I expected the match to start between 6 and 8 p.m., already not my favorite time. I prefer to play at ten in the morning instead of the evening. But on that day, it was going to be very different. The matches dragged on.

Nevertheless, I warmed up at 4 p.m. to be ready in case we were suddenly going to start. Otherwise, I spent my time reading and listening to music in the players' lounge. Many players were already finished and returning to the hotel. I was getting hungry and hadn't eaten anything for quite a while.

Around 7 p.m., the men ahead of us finally began to play. I fervently hoped they wouldn't play too long. When they started their third set, I began to warm up. It looked like a quick three-sets-to-zero match. But no, they moved on to a fourth set. I changed from my sweaty warm-up clothes into a new outfit. After all, I didn't want to get chilled. By now, my warm-up was more than six hours ago.

I asked if there was somewhere I could do a ten-minute warm-up. There was hardly anyone left at the facility; the cleaning crew was arriving. I was told I could use court 1.

After countless stairs and turns, I ended up somewhere in the cat-acombs. No one seemed to know the entrance to court 1. The men were going to their limits in the fifth set—I kept an eye on the live ticker so I would get back in time.

I could not locate court 1, and no one knew anything. After twenty-five minutes, I was back at center court, without a warm-up. The men's game was gradually coming to a close.

At 10:30 p.m., we were finally allowed to take the court. It was damn cold, no more than ten or twelve degrees Celsius. Now what? In the afternoon, I had warmed up at a pleasant twenty-five degrees Celsius. And now? I was cold and I was annoyed that I hadn't worn three-quarter-length pants instead of a thin skirt. Yesterday at that time I was already in bed.

I couldn't recall many matches I had played after 8 p.m., and even fewer that I had won—especially not against the number seven in the world. Johanna Konta seemed quite unimpressed by the situation. She appeared cheerful and present. Well, great! Now I had to find a way to perform under these difficult conditions. In the damp cold of Madrid, at 10:30 at night, without spectators.

© picture alliance, Daniel Karmann, dpa

Sports at the limit.

"No one likes it when it rains, when the weather is bad," says Bernhard Langer. "It causes a third of tournament participants to not feel motivated—and then they don't have a chance. I tend to be more of a fighter by nature and view it as a challenge."[111] You can't plan the weather, just like many other things.

---

111   Brunner (2020, pg. 48).

But how do we handle unpredictability? First, we must differentiate:

- Version 1—imaginable unfamiliar circumstances,

- Version 2—imaginable familiar circumstances,

- Version 3—completely unforeseeable circumstances.

When circumnavigator Boris Herrmann rammed a fishing boat at the *Vendeé Globe* on January 27, 2021 just before the finish, he experienced version 1, and if we consider the tragic timing, maybe even version 3.

He had sailed 50,000 kilometers in eighty days. And he was on the verge of winning the most difficult sailing regatta in the world. He had steered his sailboat past runaway containers, icebergs, sleeping whales, and then, a mere ninety kilometers from the finish, he collided with a fishing boat. All three of the alarm systems Herrmann had on board were activated, so the brief nap Hermann allowed himself was in no way negligent.

Nevertheless, and completely unforeseeably, the collision occurred during that night. No one was injured, only the boat. He was able to sail the remaining miles but at a significantly reduced speed. Herrmann still managed to maneuver his damaged "Sea Explorer" into the French destination port. He came in fifth. On the evening after his arrival, Herrmann spoke of "really bad luck," in other words, the unforeseeable, on the *ARD* program *Tagesthemen*.

Such tragic moments cannot be anticipated. We only have control over how we respond to them. Boris Herrmann accepted the situation with a fighting spirit and at least managed to take his boat across the finish line in fifth place.

If Herrmann decides to participate in the *Vendeé Globe* 2025, his starting situation will change to version 2. To the extent that one can be prepared at all for such accidents on the high seas, the familiarity of the situation would make it more imaginable.

Sure, a collision on the dark, high seas isn't completely absurd, but the total situation in Herrmann's case is.

He will factor in this experience as he prepares for the next *Vendeé Globe*. Just like—as previously mentioned—he plans to improve his handling of the grueling loneliness by learning about Buddhism.

Accepting performance fluctuations

Protecting yourself from surprises or even shocks, being able to enter a race with forethought, these things demonstrate the athletic quality of all athletes with a long sports career. They make decisions by virtue of their experience and yet still have to deal with one last unpredictable opponent: the **form of the day**.

The German downhill racer Andreas Sander placed a disappointing twenty-fourth in a downhill race in his native Garmisch-Partenkirchen in February 2021. Asked about the reason, Sander told the television station *ZDF*: "I have never been that wiped out, even though it was the shortest downhill race of the year. I think I just had a very, very bad day. It already began in the morning. I just didn't feel great, was pretty tired. I think that just happens sometimes."[112]

This illustrates that not every failure must or can be analyzed down to the last detail. Having the occasional bad day, as the Sander described, is the disadvantage humans have compared with machines.

When properly understood, the variability of daily form can also be a privilege. It releases us from the obligation to continuously bring top performances. And it thereby offers an authentic explanation for fluctuating form to everyone who has expectations of the athlete, including oneself.

---

112   Andreas Sander in a *ZDF* interview on Feb. 6, 2021.

This insight can help shorten our analysis of the recent event. Andreas Sander also quickly came to terms with his race results and looked ahead to the next goal, the Super-G on the following day: "I pretty quickly got excited about the Super-G. Completely different day. Completely different state. I feel good, I feel ready. Today is a fresh opportunity." Sander finished thirteenth. Still not completely satisfactory, but considerably better.

Every day is different, everyone should realize that. Expecting yourself to be able to bring your best every day is utopian. Rather, what sets the really good players apart is getting the best out of themselves every day within each day's possibilities.

I try to think of every upcoming match as a blank page. I want to read as little as possible into it, block out all the talk about the ranking of the two opposing players, the performances in the run-up to the match, the statistics.

To me, none of this is important in the moment before the match. I see that blank sheet of paper in front of me and it is my job to paint a picture on it using the color palette I have at my disposal today. At the same time, I know that my opponent will also try to paint her own picture with the colors she has available.

And we have to realize that there is rarely a day when everything surrounding the match goes perfectly and, on top of that, I am able to tap into all of my abilities on the court. On the contrary, usually at least one thing doesn't work at all and we have to be able to handle that skillfully.

When I'm standing on the court and the game starts, I first try to accept everything the way it is. But I don't have a detailed road-map, and from the first point on, I try to take charge of the things that are within my control and steer them in my direction. It's like there's a kind of internal scanner in the background that is providing me with a detailed image:

- *How am I feeling?*
- *What does the match feel like?*
- *What vibe am I getting from my opponent?*
- *What is her game like?*

I try to remain analytical and not waste energy on reacting emotionally to aspects that don't go the way I would like them to go. I even take it a step further and try to look at the negative things as challenges I have to overcome on this particular day.

They could be mistakes I would usually never make, well-trodden weaknesses I am all too familiar with, which are making life difficult yet again. Or they could be opportunities I needlessly squander and for which I can't forgive myself. I even view unfair calls from the referee in important moments as a challenge.

I try to maintain this mindset throughout the entire match. If I occasionally lose it, I try to regain it as quickly as possible.

And I always try to remind myself of one thing: at any time the match can still hold a positive surprise. I have experienced a lot and can honestly say, even your initial form on the day is not set in stone.

Sometimes we have a miserable start or we can lose control of three-quarters of the match. But if we fight and work on correcting mistakes, stay constructive, and continue to use our color palette to the best of our knowledge and ability, things can drastically change over the course of the match, and sometimes we get a positive surprise.

ABSORBING PRESSURE

Seven point seven million bars—that's how enormous the pressure was that scientists generated to test the resistivity of the metal osmium. The prestigious Helmholtz Association of German Research Centers tried to communicate this enormous strength to laypersons and compared this amount of pressure to "about twenty overstuffed jumbo jets balancing on one square centimeter."[113]

That sufficiently explains the scale experts think of when they talk about pressure. And what about our pressure from day-to-day moments, as well as performance in competitive sports? We cannot compete with osmium. We need a different kind of protective mechanism.

It squeezes, constricts, and won't let us breathe. Life often puts us in pressure situations. We put up resistance and lose our suppleness, our composure. But in sports, we have to be constricted and, nonetheless, cut a fine figure, a special figure, the best figure. And that is incredibly difficult.

There are so many demands pulling on the laces of our corset—the strong opponent, our own aspirations, the expectations of fans, media reports, and maybe our personal financial situation and the need to find sponsors. Parallel job- or training-related obligations also constrict. Even just reading this list makes me want to gasp for air. A quick question: what do we think of when we hear the word *pressure*?

Most likely, the answers are not that positive. But pressure can be very helpful, even essential. We can see it in a complex way in industry, particularly in energy production, and in a relaxed way in the bicycle outside our front door. When a tire has insufficient pressure, its contact surface increases, resistance grows, the bike becomes difficult to steer and to control, and riding through turns becomes risky. And doesn't the same thing happen to us in a challenging situation? Don't we also threaten to lose steerability when we go out on stage without any pressure?

---

113   Gotzner (2016).

When there isn't enough pressure or I don't feel a sufficient amount of pressure, it can have a negative effect. There is no tension, and the activation level remains too low for the impending task.

During my career, there have been only a few matches when I was barely or not at all nervous. While I appreciated being extremely relaxed at the moment before the match started, I ended up not playing well because I was unable to achieve my necessary activation level. There is no way around it: You must be fully present, physically and mentally, and feel the importance and relevance of the task at hand to be able to achieve an optimal performance.

"Pressure makes diamonds," is the title of Christoph Kittler's professional article in the magazine *Zeitschrift für Sportpsychologie*.[114] So, pressure creates masters. Some tasks require unconditional peak performance under immense pressure.

Take the surgeon who, without delay, must operate on the patient just arriving at the emergency department with the ambulance siren wailing. It could be a matter of life and death. The surgical instruments must be put to work quickly and precisely; for the rescuer, there is no time to rest. Rescuing people from drowning, being buried by an avalanche, being trapped in a cave, or rescuing them from a burning building puts support staff under enormous pressure in terms of time and quality. Disarming bombs, making an emergency landing with an airplane—the list of professional moments that are challenging in every way is endless.

Even without lives being under threat, the pressure of time alone always sets the pace for professional actions—the project that must be completed to meet a tight deadline, or the eloquent media release that should be completed immediately after a result to be posted online. Or the decisive penalty shot in the World Cup final, the leader coming last in the

---

114   Kittler (2019, pg. 142).

biathlon competition, or the match point that must be defended as the end of a five-hour tennis match approaches.

Learning to perform under pressure is more than a logical consequence, at work, in sports, and during a challenge. So, let's begin with a differentiated look at pressure.

External pressure: Expectations are placed on me. Hence, I have something to prove to fans, my family, my own team, friends, competitors, and the media. Off the court, there's lots of fuss and lots of stress, press conferences, recording a clip here, and holding an autograph session.

While preparing for important matches, I can feel the self-imposed pressure increase. That takes us to internal pressure: whether as an athlete or in some other area, performance is generally preceded by a preparation phase. I have invested lots of time and energy and now want to reward myself, preferably with a top performance.

It was most likely the pressure that got to Novak Djokovic in 2021, when he failed to win the "Golden Slam," winning all four Grand Slam tournaments in the same year, including a gold medal at the Olympics. To date, Steffi Graf has been the only one to accomplish this major coup, back in 1988.

Djokovic, number one in the world, was off to a fantastic start having secured the first Grand Slam title of the year in Melbourne, the second one in Paris, and the third victory at Wimbledon. But he lost against Alexander Zverev in the semi-final at the Olympics.

The pressure then erupted in highly expressive fashion during his bronze-medal match against the Spaniard Pablo Careño. Djokovic angrily threw his racket into the empty stands and later smashed another racket on the court.

The amount of value and pressure associated with record-setting and achieving legend status became apparent once more later that same year, when Djokovic, in tears, lost the US Open final, the fourth Grand Slam contest of the year, against Daniil Medvedev.

> *Pressure has a distinct physical effect. It can leave me breathless before a major task; it can make me feel like the tension has crept into every fiber of my body. Sometimes it can even make you feel paralyzed and deny you your body's own resources. The ability to control activation level, coordination, and the ability to recuperate is then just as limited as freshness and speed.*
>
> *There are athletes who thrive on this wave of discomfort. But most will consider this type of tension as rather unpleasant and something that adds mental pressure in addition to the physical.*

We must therefore consider our relationship with pressure.

- How much pressure can we handle?

- How much pressure do we require to function really well?

- And why do we not strive to completely control our pressure?

Let's go back briefly to the plausibility of tire pressure. Earlier, we compared the progression of a match or tournament to a journey. Not a journey that we wouldn't check the tire pressure beforehand, since we value our personal safety. We wouldn't even think of letting the pressure take care of itself. Just too dangerous.

That same principle should come to mind during an important moment in sports: we do not relinquish control over the pressure! Because that would cause us to lose some control over our game.

Let's take one of the most exciting situations in soccer. It's the knock-out round, normal playing time is over, as is extra time. Now it's down to penalty shots. Both teams have five penalty shots at their disposal. Goal: maximum yield. Situation: maximum pressure. Regulation: only when the referee releases the ball with a whistle is the player allowed to run toward the ball and take the shot.

And now comes the moment when we briefly pause our analysis and take a detached look at the scene. We put ourselves in the place of the penalty-taker: the referee blows the whistle, meaning he releases the ball, and the player can now take the shot, but it does not mean he has to do so as quickly as possible.

Yet reality shows that the whistle incites many players to start to run immediately. But that only applies to the whistle-like starting gun in track and field. It is not the case with the soccer penalty kick. Of course, the player must approach the ball in a timely manner, but not immediately.

Securing decision-making authority

Once I understand this, I gain a little time to focus without being interrupted by a whistle. And, most notably, I achieve authority over my time management and thereby regain some authority over my actions.

We can turn this into a general mantra; in other words, whenever possible, set the beat ourselves. This pattern of rushing into action can be seen in many of life's situations. We humans have an internal trigger that impels us to react quickly. Sometimes, we aren't capable of letting a question go unanswered, even for more than a couple of seconds.

The person who answers the fastest often wins. It's better to bridge a silence with an "er" than take the time for contemplation. Saying nothing seems to be equated with knowing nothing. Here, life can give us the freedom to be a little more relaxed.

Withstanding extraordinary pressure

The more regulators I can control from my control center, the better. Because situations with lots at stake also demand a lot from me. My attentiveness and movement automation are at risk of being impaired.

Back in the 1980s, the American psychologist Roy Baumeister described **choking under pressure**,[115] as a drop in performance that results from a situation that demands a particularly good performance. Moments like this occur, for instance, in final games or when spectators have extremely high expectations.

This paralyzing effect has been the focus of many studies. Financial incentive has also been shown to have a negative effect. The more money at stake, the more likely it is that the performance will decline.[116] Add to that a strong **loss aversion**—meaning a tendency to view losses as weightier than wins—and the situation becomes even more precarious and the ability to bring the usual performance even more questionable.

It is essential to understand all of this and deepen that understanding by talking with a sports psychologist. Years of competitive experience can sometimes help as well. Magdalena Neuner talks about the phase when she entered the World Cup at a very young age. "I thought the world would come to an end when I took a bad shot and people would think I didn't have what it takes. I sometimes felt that way for days afterwards. The demands, the fans, the external pressure, the interviews—all of it overwhelmed me."

The pressure quickly gains momentum and, particularly as a young athlete, mentally keeping up with the old hands is challenging. Some of this can be addressed during the training process with **immunization training, prognosis training, and uniqueness training.**[117]

---

115   Baumeister (1984).
116   Dunne et al. (2018, pg. 19).
117   Beckman & Elbe (2008, pg. 120f).

Pressure must be simulated in training and acclimatization, in other words, immunization must be encouraged. I am able to ambitiously project and manifest my hits during shooting practice while specifying actions in case I miss. Furthermore, I end the training session with a non-repeatable and therefore one-time task given to me by the trainer without previous announcement.

The effect of the unfamiliar and unpracticed lies outside of our control and overwhelms us. The excessive demand then quickly affects our concentration and coordination. It becomes difficult to stop the drop in performance.

Always having to achieve something, always playing for certain results, always functioning and training in a certain way—that is how I put a lot of pressure on myself during the first half of my career. I have always given it my all, always tried to train more, put in more time, and work harder than everyone else.

But over time, this mentality of always putting that much pressure on myself limited my creativity and my enthusiasm in the sport and in my private life. There was already barely any free time due to the huge demands of my daily work, and when I did have some free time, I was too exhausted to enjoy it. The balance was off, but I thought that's what it took to become successful.

It was a crucial moment in my career when I shifted the mental focus in my sport on feeling more joy and passion. I was able to view good performances and results as a bonus. A lot of pressure has fallen away as a result and I was able to really come into my own.

WILD CARD

Acting against our own feelings is rarely productive. That is also the assessment of *Eurosport* expert Werner Schuster. He knows what he's talking about. For many years he was the successful coach of the German national ski-jumping team. "When he tries to compensate with courage it usually gets even worse," was his comment on Stefan Kraft's jump on the fourth competition day of the Four Hills Tournament. "It goes better when you take a relaxed jump. The worst thing for the athlete is when he has to jump against his instinct."[118] Kraft is from Austria and an Olympic champion and four-time world champion.

Unless it is against the actual opponent, going "against" something is generally not inspiring and robs you of energy. The previously described fight against one's feelings, the fight against one's own perception, against lack of motivation, effort, one's weaker self, against pain, against fear, against pressure should all be kept manageable and episodic.

Permanence becomes a problem. At worst, long-term, excessive pressure ends in failure. Ultimately, the pressure can penetrate the soul to a point that the ripcord must be pulled. Soccer coach Ralf Rangnick had to pull hard. "I have nothing left,"[119] was the headline in the newspaper *Bild-Zeitung* in September 2011. Successful trainer suffers from **burnout**. The fact that the media, especially the tabloid press, also follow these events with great interest, of course, does nothing to aid rehabilitation.

But that is the lot of the elite athlete. We have chosen this place in the world and, at a certain level, we become a public figure. That is a term from civil law. It is impossible to avoid. The quality and the scope of the tasks and responsibilities increase as the performance level goes up.

---

118   Werner Schuster with *Eurosport*, Jan. 5, 2022, fourth jump at the Four Hills Tournament 2021/2022 in Bischofshofen.
119   Wenzel & Kitsch (2011).

Like sick people, those who are injured also get little rest. That makes the convalescent sensitive, almost anxious. An athlete returning from an extended injury layoff worries that the spectators will compare every one of his moves mercilessly with the performance of the player who had temporarily taken his place. And maybe he is right.

But it is just as likely that the fans will be excited that the athlete made it back to the team and onto the field after their injury, and they may even forgive the occasional mistake. Both spectator attitudes are very likely. Allowing yourself this point of view lightens your load a lot.

Valuing pressure

Pressure can also be something completely different: a privilege. In the words of Billy Jean King, the tennis legend who won thirty-nine Grand Slam titles in singles, doubles, and mixed doubles and success-fully advanced emancipation in tennis: "Great moments carry great weight—that is what pressure to perform is all about. And though it can be tough to face that kind of pressure, very few people get the chance to experience it."[120]

As overwhelming and unpleasant as pressure may feel, on the one hand, it should also be viewed as an exceptional opportunity that few get to experience. And remembering how much outstanding work one must have accomplished to get this special opportunity completes the change in perspective. Or might it even be a paradigm shift?

---

120   King (2008, pg. 101).

When the feeling of pressure gets to be so big that I fear it may interfere with my ability to tap into my potential, I sometimes remember the words: "Pressure is privilege!"

I tell myself: If this moment wasn't so incredibly important, I wouldn't feel such pressure. And if I hadn't played so well, I wouldn't even be here. The moment is an opportunity, not a burden, even if it feels like one. The moment is so difficult that I may rise above myself and go a step further than I might have thought possible.

PROCESSING ERRORS AND FAILURE

Let's begin with the highly regarded **positive emotion**. It gives us wings, lets us lose ourselves in it, and makes us proud. It can shift our own expectations, but at its worst can also lead to overestimating ourselves. At the least, it entails the risk of confidently setting our bar too high and even knocking it down if we hang it too high. We have to come to grips with that. Only then will we avoid falling victim to the flood of our own emotions.

But **negative** emotions cause us far more problems—when we fall behind, when nothing goes as planned, or when everything is different than usual. It begins inconspicuously, with slight disappointment and grows, if we let it, into worry, then moves seamlessly into frustration, and ends up as a grueling tandem of anger and despair. When anger builds up and looms over us like a mountain, we've already let it go too far.

The longer we let negative emotions affect us, the more they tug and pull at us: missed scoring opportunities in soccer, missed shots in biathlon, double faults in tennis—every sport has its typical heart-stopping moments, which, seen individually, are unpleasant enough. Once they gain a foothold, it becomes difficult to get rid of them. Thus, the stream of thoughts must be outmaneuvered before it accelerates. Because when the mind is still focused on that missed shot, our reaction speed decreases, our backward movement on the field is likely delayed, and an alert opponent will exploit the situation.

Also, when the biathlon athlete misses the target with the first shot, self-doubt can creep into the consciousness and impair concentration for the subsequent shots. And as long as frustration about the double fault during the tennis serve is still going through our head, it will, of course, work against a precise next serve.

Some athletes then need a quick outlet, such as the Australian tennis player Nick Kyrgios. His anger—in this case not directed at himself but at the chair umpire—drove him to the changing room at the 2019 Cincinnati tournament, where he smashed two rackets and then returned to the court. It did not help him; he lost the decisive third set 2:6.

It was even less beneficial later that year at the Rome tournament when he threw a plastic chair onto the court in exasperation. He was disqualified. At the preparatory tournament for the 2021 Australian Open, he not only smashed a racket but subsequently threw it out of the stadium. He lost that match as well.

Nevertheless, the example of this particular tennis personality shows that there is an inner urge to vent one's anger. We can see this again and again in tennis, either via impulsive shouts born from frustration or frequently thrown rackets. Cautions and money fines are either forgotten in the transport of one's own impetuousness or are simply accepted. It is an intuitive desire for internal cleansing.

Although this form of eccentricity is occasionally successful, scientists warn that getting upset can lead to disastrous results because emotional reactions can impact concentration and subsequent decisions for another twenty minutes.[121]

---

121   Beckmann & Elbe (2008, pg. 121).

© picture alliance, Daniel Bockwoldt, dpa

Obligated to win, sacrificed to frustration.

Twenty minutes! Twenty minutes can change the world. The force of environmental catastrophes can be felt in minutes, often in seconds. Gas leaks or toxic chemicals, oil spills, firestorms, tsunamis, and volcanic eruptions only take moments to change the world.

Fauna, flora, and often people can fall victim to these moments. Mere minutes can decide whether or not someone survives a heart attack. There is hardly a James Bond movie whose plot doesn't involve a race against time, taking viewers along to the second as the clock runs down. As this brief digression into life-threatening events shows, time is an immense factor that we would love to be able to control.

But timing is often a matter of luck, coincidence, fate. Brief moments can turn into huge disasters. Austrian Marcel Hirscher got off lightly in December 2015 when a drone filming the slalom race crashed onto the course right behind him, maybe by hundredths of a second, instead of shattering on his head. Many of the Formula One accidents had less fortunate endings. In events such as these, timing ignores us and plays its own game.

But then there is the kind of timing we control, that we practice. All artistic and aesthetic sports live by their precise timing, just like the Kempa—or even the double-Kempa—trick in handball, as well as the stop in badminton or tennis.

And then there are moments when established time patterns are simply ditched. There was such a moment in September 2015. It lasted nine minutes. That's how long it took Bayern Munich striker Robert Lewandowski to score five goals for his legendary five-pack. And it happened incredibly fast in 1988, when Steffi Graf won the shortest Grand Slam final. She defeated the number 12 seed Natallja Swerawa at the French Open in just thirty-two minutes.

From the tennis court to the chess board: during a blitz chess game, players have only ten minutes to think. Not to mention mere seconds for javelin throws, upward circles on the high bar, ski jumps, and 100-meter sprints.

This more than illustrates the immense time span of those twenty minutes that one might need to recover from particularly loud angry eruptions. That applies to sports as well as professional decision-making situations. Sensibly channeling those emotions as quickly as possible is fundamental.

But penetrating the complicated maze of our thoughts isn't quite that easy. Distorted perception is typical after a moment of frustration. For instance, a good performance might be downplayed to an average performance, and a normal performance might be considered a failure. Another frequent reaction is self-pity, sometimes even self-loathing.

A hot microphone at the 2007 Australian Open in Melbourne captured the legendary self-talk of Tommy Haas. He was down by one set against the Russian Nikolay Davydenko in the quarter final, he had just lost his service, and it was a change of ends.

Ego kick via self-criticism

"You can't win like that. You can't win like that, Haasi, it won't work," he berated himself. "This simply won't do. This simply won't do. Just too weak. Too many errors, too many errors. It's always the same. I don't want to do it anymore. Why am I doing this shit? For what? For whom? Except for myself, right? Why? Why? What for? I can't do it; I don't get it. I pay people for nothing, for absolutely nothing. Just so I can get upset. You're a complete idiot. You didn't go to the net again."[122]

Then the referee announced the change of ends. And Tommy Haas? Within seconds he took off his old frustration personality, threw it on the bench, and pulled on his new motivation outfit with the words: "But you're going to win! Come on, you'll win this. You can't lose. Fight. Fight. Fight!" He encouraged himself with this announcement and went on to the next match.

He immediately played a fabulous winner in the subsequent rally and ultimately won the set and, in the end, the match.

122   Barschel (2015).

Former number one tennis player Angelique Kerber also talks to herself self-mockingly. But doing so does not provide a prognosis for the remainder of the match.

In September 2021, she faced off against Leylah Fernandez in the round of sixteen at the US Open. While she did lose, it was a very classy match. And Barbara Ritter, the *Eurosport* expert, commented on Kerber's frustration with the words: "When her stubbornness comes out, so does her swing."

The national coach thereby called attention to a potentially positive link between disgruntled self-criticism and successful tennis-playing. Magdalena Neuner can attest to that: "Turning aggression and anger into something positive releases unbelievable powers in me. It works really well on the course."

This does not mean that the sports psychologist tends to encourage positive and goal-oriented self-talk directed at the future. Rather, it becomes apparent, first of all, how differently individuals function, and secondly, that a single individual can react very differently depending on the day and the circumstances.

And precisely that is our takeaway: that our ability to adhere to a strict formula in mental training is conditional. Every individual needs a customized plan, and even that requires frequent adjustments with the creative willingness to strike new paths.

The best example of that mentioned diversity is communication in team sports. While one player is motivated by, "It doesn't matter, the next ball finds its mark," another needs to be loudly reprimanded. It's not easy knowing which form of encouragement would be helpful to the teammate at that moment in the hectic, fast-moving game.

In coaching athletes, one will naturally try to make the athlete independent of the preferences of others. The goal is to develop an athlete with a self-sufficient, stable, or at least resilient attitude in moments of failure.

Being able to lose is one of the most important lessons I have learned over the course of my career. Our losses are often our own fault, and we must have the ability to be hard on ourselves, to learn from our mistakes, and make the necessary adjustments. Here it is very important to be honest with yourself and remain objective in your self-analysis. And to know the difference between a mistake we made and when the opponent was simply too good.

Making excuses and putting the blame on external circumstances is a big mistake, and by doing so, you deprive yourself of an opportunity to grow. But it's just as bad to not respect the competitor's performance and blame the loss entirely on your own shortcomings. By doing so, you torpedo your own self-worth and get in the way of your own progress.

To me, being able to lose means being able to analyze and differentiate between my own performance and the opponent's and to draw constructive conclusions for the future.

The mind can help regulate emotions, but so can the body. A drop in performance also manifests itself in the latter and is often visible on the outside. Of course, we want to prevent any obvious signs as they would empower the opponent; they would practically shout out that this would be a good time to convert that rebound.

But a closed body cannot hide what is going on inside. And the closed body denies my view into the distance, my target, and also my opponent. My view is limited; I am trapped in time and place.

Samy Molcho, the probably most renowned expert on **body language**, said: "We trigger reactions with every movement we make."[123] This factor can be used to manipulate the opponent, for instance, by making

---

123   Molcho (1988, pg. 189).

the body bigger from the start, regardless of your own self-perception, pushing out the chest, looking straight ahead with a superior smile.

But this factor can also be used to correct our own demeanor, by (and this is not an accidental repetition of words) making the body big, pushing out the chest, and looking straight ahead with a superior smile regardless of your own self-perception.

© picture alliance, Filip Singer, dpa

When body language leaves no doubt as to the inner attitude.

As far back as 1971, the US psychologist Albert Mehrabian was able to show in a study that people relay 55 percent of information via facial expressions.[124] This can be seen in the expression of a tennis player when he makes up a point deficit and scores the critical point: determination. And the clenched fist—it is impossible for the opponent to miss this victory-focused and hormone-driven expression.

- A level 1 strategy would be to maintain a poker face to keep the opponent from seeing your hand: an unchanging facial expression as a sign of consistency and resilience.

- Level 2 would be playing with posture and facial expression, in other words, consciously masking frustration. This would cause the opponent to become irritated but, as previously mentioned, it would also initiate you righting yourself literally and figuratively.

Monika Matschnig, former player on the Austrian national volleyball team and a psychologist, specializes in body language and rates an upright head position as confident and neutral. An exercise she recommends is to imagine that you're balancing a book on top of your head or placing a book there and walking.[125]

What matters is maintaining body tension to avoid losing control over your emotions. An accompanying measure can be maintaining the flow of movement and "not getting distracted by intrusive thoughts, but remaining action- and task-focused."[126]

Science refers to this very important interplay between body and mind as **embodiment**. Self-confidence can be reinforced by righting the person in the literal sense. Just like the body slumps during a phase of weakness, it rights itself in a situation of strength. That is precisely the point, according to the German Spa and Physical Therapy Center, when

---

124   Mehrabian (1971, pg. 43).
125   Matschnig (2007, pg. 22).
126   Beckmann-Waldenmayer & Beckmann (2012, pg. 124).

successful intervention is possible by taking advantage of the link between mental state and physical expression.

The mind affects the body, so why can't the body affect the mind? Consciously righting yourself, maybe even puffing out the chest, triggers a response that impacts the entire body. The change in sight distance also helps. Someone who previously only looked at the ground, with his head held high can now see the depth of the world.

Body language can absolutely be trained, and not just through conscious realization but also through visualization. Lukas Kampa, player on the German national volleyball team and four-time volleyball player of the year, helped himself by imagining that he saw himself playing a game on television.[127]

Visualization becomes even more realistic when we film ourselves. Because video analysis, which has long been used for technical and tactical feedback, shows the situation exactly as it is, meaning it does not permit any idealization as can happen when working strictly with the imagination.

Letting the body speak

Let's take a handball team for instance. The goal of appearing certain of victory, combative, even aggressive, must emanate from every fiber in the body from the first second of the game, ideally even during the warm-up. The synergy between the individual players can create an aura that frightens the opponent and quickly overwhelms him. Nothing reveals the ability to make such a physical presence visible like video clip.

Here we will briefly shift our focus to the trainer. He also contributes with his body language and not just with announcements, encouragement, or abuse.

---

127 Gatzmaga et al. (2020, pg. 14).

WILD CARD

Let's imagine a handball coach who watches the game sitting down. The coach sends out different messages to the one who wildly gesticulates from the sidelines. There are appropriate moments for both behaviors. What matters is reflecting on what happens when and why.

And the bench must also be taken into consideration to complete the team analysis. They, too, can contribute to the team's aura by making their body bigger and thereby forcing respect from the opponents. Every single player, whether on the field or on the bench, adds something in the team by radiating self-confidence.

Oliver Kahn and Manuel Neuer in the soccer goal, Johannes Bitter and Andreas Wolff in the handball goal, all world-class players, provide the best example and demonstrate how a sense of calm and authority envelopes the team from back to front as an empowering energy corset.

To regulate emotions, Beckmann & Elbe[128] recommend combining cognitive and physical measures. With the body: remain upright, head held high, calm breaths with slow exhalation. With cognition: analyze failures and encourage relief measures.

When frustration is particularly severe, simple but strenuous movements can help build up catecholamines such as epinephrine, norepinephrine, and cortisol. Such a movement could be a practice swing in golf as a substitute for the frustration scream into the woods, which is frowned upon on a golf course anyway.

Regulating emotions cannot just be successfully achieved via the detour that is the body. We can also activate the mind directly, for instance with self-talk: "Mistake, bam, gone!" That would be the ideal formula for quickly forgetting a mishap and initiating a new action. Mistake, bam, gone. It would only take a second, and generally there isn't more processing time than that.

Unfortunately, we tend to function based on the principle of mistake-bam-shock and store all of the mishaps as unpleasant whisperers in

128   Beckmann & Elbe (2008, pg. 121).

the back of our head. One important step to counter this uninvited prompter: we must **forgive ourselves** as we should forgive others.

When we forgive, we make the decision to "let our grudge peter out,"[129] said Susanne Boshammer in an interview. The Professor of Practical Philosophy at Osnabrück University named the keyword: grudge. When we allow ourselves to hold a grudge, we become distracted, lose control over our attentiveness. Our performance is bound to suffer. And when we are unable to bring a decent performance, sooner or later we begin to doubt ourselves.

Wherever the solution-focused future-oriented word is uttered, no room remains for disappointed hindsight. The solution formula by Henning Fritz is concise and forward-looking: "Looking at a spot for three seconds and then moving on to the thought for the next situation."

There is also little room for general skepticism. Sometimes we have to go further afield and briefly overhype the situation by asking ourselves why we are even on the court, in the stadium, or on the pitch. What fundamental motive drives us to stand here to compete?

CONSTRUCTIVE MIND GAMES

At the 2008 Olympics in Peking, German world-class swimmer Britta Steffen simply tricked her ears.[130] In her mind, she turned spectator cheers of "China, China" into "Britta, Britta." She also visualized the racing dive as a catapult. In the pool she thought of herself as swimming with dolphins and during the turn she turned into a ball of lightning. She used the image of a feather for the subsequent push-off, and for the clutch on the home stretch, Britta Steffen imagined being pursued by a small shark. In Peking she won Olympic gold in the 50 and 100 meters, and for years was the fastest female swimmer in the world.

---

129   Hauschild (2020).
130   Catuogno (2019).

WILD CARD

The power of imagery does not only matter in advertising but also in optimizing our own performance—not only at the movie theater around the corner but also in the one inside our head. It is fortunate that we are already experienced in this form of visualized exertion of influence.

- Because how often do we mentally review situations in life—anticipating a job interview, a salary negotiation, a first date?

- What am I going to say?

- How will my counterpart respond?

- What will my facial expression be?

- What will I wear?

Everyday scripts are often created in our head, most often intuitively, but occasionally strategically prepared like a chess game.

And that's how we can approach it and create a script that focuses on performance development. We are both the director and leading actor and have free rein with the implementation. We can be a ball of lightning and a feather like Britta Steffen. Or anything else our image of a leading actor inspires.

And mental imagery is very effective, not least because humans require only about one tenth of a second to register the basic content of a photo.[131]

And there's a second, highly relevant visualization training aspect. Namely, that we are able to also use our imagination to inject an optimized

---

131 Digital photo (2018)

motion sequence. As the legendary snowboarder Shaun White supposedly said, he had already nailed all of the jumps in his head while in the start hut.[132] Now he would just have to do them.

- And when the images in our head are incorrect?

- How do we expel optical garbage from our system?

Being a good director in your own head cinema

"That is one of the most difficult tasks in golf," says Bernhard Langer. "I remember well when as a nineteen-year-old I was leading on the final day of the Irish Open, back then one of the biggest tournaments on the calendar. Nine holes to go with a two-hole lead."

Langer was new on the circuit. He was not yet familiar with winning tournaments. He made his tenth drive. "It was wonderful. I walked the 250 meters to the ball and for the first time I thought: What are you going to do about the thousands of spectators standing at the eighteenth green? And then you have to give a speech in front of a huge crowd, which I had never done before. My next thought was: What are you going to do with all that prize money you will win here? Will you buy a car? Invest in the stock market? Three holes later I was no longer in the lead. I played bogies and the other players pars and birdies. I did not win the tournament."[133]

This resulted in a consequence many successful top athletes live: "The only thing that matters is the next shot." It is about the great art of directing one's attention, of focusing one's concentration. Gerd Schönfelder, 16-time Paralympic champion and hobby golfer, agrees with Bernhard Langer: "Focusing on that one ball while simultaneously ignoring everything else around you, is good practice. In general, for daily life as a disabled person."

---

132 Eurosport, Feb. 9, 2022.
133 Brunner (2020, pg. 48).

Looking back, biathlete Magdalena Neuner confirms this as well: "When you're not 100 percent focused, you go belly-up. I always loved that about my sport: having to ignore everything else if you want to do well."

In December 2020, the biathlete Franziska Preuss said after the ten-kilometer pursuit race in Hochfilzen: "At the first standing position I didn't notice a thing. At the last one I might not have had complete tunnel vision. I could hear the stadium announcer. And that's always a bad sign." That prevented her from refocusing herself. "Of course, it's annoying when you end up shooting two errors."[134]

Sometimes, when I lose my focus, I use a technique I once learned from a mental coach. For instance, when I sit on the bench during the change of ends, I deliberately vary my perceptual focus from broad to very narrow and back again.

I then consciously allow all extraneous noise, the things I would otherwise ignore. I absorb the noise from spectators going to the restroom during the break, I hear how they noisily climb up and down the stands. I pay attention to the hiss of the water when the court is sprayed down, and I notice the din from the VIP section at the front of the court where people are turning their afternoon at the tennis court into a champagne party and watch our match on the side.

Then I try to narrow my focus lightning-fast to just myself. Everything I just mentioned is blocked out and I feel only my body and my breath, try to focus on just me in a quiet bubble. Once I've managed to do so, I switch back to a broad focus, and then switch back and forth several times.

This exercise is like a short version of what I will shortly need during my match when my focus should drift.

---

134   ZDF interview, Dec. 13, 2020.

© picture alliance, dpa

It's all about the head: focus as the basis of a good performance.

Such a simple and certainly helpful tool against uncontrolled roaming thoughts simply stops these thoughts. Constructing a visual barrier in the form of a roadblock, gate, or stop sign can trigger this effect.

We are familiar with another measure from the game *Monopoly*—"Return to start," and from the cellphone manual—"Return to factory setting." We reset ourselves to zero like the daily mileage display in our car. We persuade ourselves to start over. Uninhibited. Past errors, shots, passes, throws—they never happened. The first three holes in golf—foul ball, water, three-putt. Reset: I basically start from scratch, at hole number four.

I will deal with the analysis of the original start of the round tonight, that much athletic ambition is essential. As Eberspächer says, use the break as a lock.[135] A space between two systems that you can use for a kind of cleansing to start the next segment in an optimized state.

When things get particularly tight at the end of a match, when every point is critical and the nerves of all involved on and off the court are already raw, I try a trick to stay relaxed and loose in my head with my decision-making perceptions and movement execution.

I sometimes imagine that the score at the beginning of the first set is 2:2. How would I play? How unfettered would I feel during my shots? How would I trust my intuition if there wasn't so much at stake? I try to conjure up this feeling and carry it with me to the next point while also staying highly focused.

135   Eberspächer (2012, pg. 98).

Unfortunately, taking our thoughts on such dream trips isn't always that easy. What to do with all our attentiveness? Which trains of thought are beneficial? The US sports psychologist Robert M. Nideffer first brought some order to this confusion in the 1960s and divided attentiveness into four dimensions. Here, narrow and wide as well as internal and external are aligned at opposite ends.[136]

His "attention diagram" shows these four combinations:

• Broad and directed inward.

• Broad and directed outward.

• Narrow and directed inward.

• Narrow and directed outward.

Certain sports and certain game situations can be matched to specific forms of attention. In more complex sports, those players who are able to access different dimensions appropriately have an advantage. But first let's look at each one separately:

• Wide and directed inward (broad internal): These are the analytical ones who mentally go through the game before the game. They learn and adapt and rarely make the same mistake twice. They anticipate the actions of their opponents. They adequately adjust their own style. That can be both a major strength and a great weakness. They are often so caught up in their own analysis that they experience anything else as a surprise and occasionally overestimate themselves.

• Broad and directed outward (broad external): Suitable for rapidly changing game situations. Everything that happens around this type must penetrate the consciousness. Typical athlete with an eye for the open player in soccer or basketball. Becomes problematic when there is a major influx of information.

---

136   Nideffer (1967, pg. 52 et seq.).

- Narrow and directed inward (narrow internal): Focus on that one thought. Helpful when it's about a single intensive action, such as in weightlifting. Able to control the mental component of pain. It's like being at a dentist who distracts us from thinking about pain with music. Some athletes are able to achieve that feat by shifting their focus on, for instance, the swinging arm or the breathing rhythm. But even when pain tolerance can be increased, ultimately everything comes down to the strength of the self-concept.

- Narrow and directed outward (narrow external): The more precise a movement has to be, the narrower the focus must be. Great concentration on details. This helps prevent unnecessary distractions. A good example is putting in golf. Athletes are not irritated by noise or fans standing too close to the field. They are not distracted by their own thoughts since they are outward-focused. It's problematic when the game requires flexibility and change. Sometimes lack expanded field information.

Being familiar with these facets of attention is helpful, but it's even better to be able to apply them appropriately and variably. Many sports—as well as life situations—cannot be managed with just *one* dimension.

Let's take golf, for instance. A player's focus has to be broad and external to register distances and possible wind and use that knowledge to choose the right club. We must become broad and internal to match the gathered information to our own capabilities, for example, how one played at the last competition under the same conditions—more conservative or bold?

Then we choose the club and our focus changes to narrow and external, meaning it is focused on the ball. After the shot, we need the narrow internal aspect to mentally revisit what happened and how we felt, which mistakes we must analyze.

In any team sport, players must be able to constantly alternate between all four dimensions. This applies in a panel discussion or a board meeting, too. The speaker must know, and be able to use, the four attention categories. We cannot assume that someone can use all dimensions equally well. That is why they have to be practiced.

The sphere that is particularly worthy of protection is concentration as it is expressed in the two "narrow" dimensions. In a circle graph, Eberspächer shows how "I" get distracted from the outside in my task fulfillment (see fig. 1).

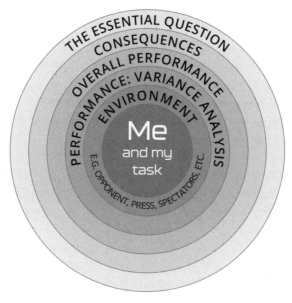

Fig. 1: Influences on concentration in a sports context (Eberspächer, 2012, pg. 46)

SELF-TALK

The swimmer Britta Steffen previously revealed that we don't need a human counterpart for an exchange of ideas. She made water her dialogue partner. It's a clever idea to find something you spend so much time with for the dialogue. But it can also be done without water, without any external means. It can be done with just yourself.

So, I can have a discourse with myself, which has the major advantage that my dialogue partner is ever-present.

WILD CARD

When I make a good connection with myself, I have valuable guidance available around the clock.

Now there is the herculean task of making myself a reliable adviser. In reality, we are unfortunately often a very destructive dialogue partner and berate ourselves for mishaps: "You moron!," "I just don't get it!," "Darn game!," "Nothing works today!," "What is up with that?" You don't need a college degree to know that such a negative exchange with yourself is useless and even harmful.

Our first insight: We are already familiar with self-talk and use it intuitively, but apparently we know little about beneficial content. Which self-talk formula is most effective depends on the individual. There is some benefit from the previously mentioned thought or shouted "Come on!," while others benefit more from explicitly reminding themselves of their strengths.

Not advisable are formulas with negative language such as "Don't be . . . !," "Don't do . . . !," "Don't have . . . !," "I can't do it!" It's funny, but in that moment of agitation we become the greatest dilettantes, losers, even idiots.

The often intuitively added "again and again" or "like always" is also counterproductive. Too much self-doubt. It is obvious that this disqualifying self-condemnation should be turned into solution-oriented instructions packaged in short sentences with prompts, ideally in first person.

Any vocabulary with a negative connotation should be banished from these phrases. A "No one is as bad as I am," gets radically shredded. The new formulas are: I will transition quicker!" and "I will take the ball earlier!"

And it's also best to leave out the hinted-at comparison to the unsuccessful past and eliminate the nearly invisible but important "-er" at the end of the word. Instead of "faster" and "earlier" it will be: "I will transition quickly!" and "I'll take the ball early!" That is how our strategy **convinces us of the self-efficacy** we need so much to succeed.

Our self-instruction requires a sensible direction, a motive with substance. When we take that into consideration, we get motivating formulas. Then we can tell ourselves things that:

* Give us courage: "You can do this!"

* Help us gain perspective: "Done. Move on!"

* Give us praise: "Perfect shot!"

* Help us focus: "Eyes on the ball!"

* Offer a solution: "Mark the inside lane!"

* Show us an action-oriented direction: "Play the next volley backhand!"

Writing your own script

Every negative slogan tends to have a positive counterpart. And the negative troublemakers are easily identified. All we have to do is write down the phrases we direct at ourselves during the competition. Afterwards, we should look at each assertion and check it for its constructive potential. We adapt, change, rewrite, and create a script that has, at least, a chance of a happy ending.

Positive, productive, and action-oriented is how a "valuable inner dialogue" is created, just like W. Timothy Gallwey emphasizes in his now famous books on the psyche and golf and tennis players.[137]

The now popular **mindfulness techniques** also focus on helpful language for self-analysis. One of the basic ideas is to perceive your feelings but not to assess them.

---

137   Gallwey (1981/2012).

A "I am uncertain," is substituted by a "That is uncertainty." This change in the level helps us in two ways:

- First, we distance ourselves from a bad feeling,

- And second, we express that there are other, also positive feelings.[138]

It's about dealing with burdensome feelings in a constructive way.

This approach should not have the dubious aura of self-deceit. That deceit would, at most, be some small, psychologically legitimate self-deceit. The slogan "Fake it till you make it," exists for a reason. We help ourselves with a little ruse and regulate our mental goings-on.

When we provide therapy to the body of that slumped, bent-over person with their drooping shoulders and hunched back, raise them up and encourage them to push out their chest—we will give a nudge. We won't cure depression, but we will show them that next to the despondency, there is something else, and we do that by demonstrating to the inner feeling of sadness a feeling of confidence and greatness that can be felt on the outside.

We can also use the inner dialogue to gain a better perspective that replaces the negative with a positive view. Because that almost always exists. In the best-case scenario, it can be accompanied by an objective analysis as well as a subjective mental health analysis.[139]

As the saying goes, "It is in the eye of the beholder."

It's a good idea to create a "training journal of prohibited sentences." For a designated period of time, after each training session I record what I say to myself in critical situations. For example, in handball, I record

---

138   Staufenbiel et al. (2019, pg. 165).
139   Eberspächer (2012, pg. 91).

when I miss a throw, play a bad pass, make a sloppy catch, don't react quickly enough, defend halfheartedly, stand in the circle, when my teammate makes a mistake in a practice game, and when the coach reprimands me.

The sentences are in the left column, and the right column shows my phrasing challenge. For every backward-looking negative statement in the left column, new solution- and action-oriented phrasing is needed in the right column. "How could you miss that?" is turned into "I will jump further into the circle with the next ball!"

This I-message with action orientation has the power to influence me in a positive way. Some of these sentences can then be added to my archive. In the end, the right column has managed to eliminate the left one.

Internalized self-talk for the competition

What works during training should also be automated in good time during competitions. But not every competition dialogue can be programmed. Rather, the motivating self-talk must be internalized as a valuable blueprint. Those who struggle with quick and situation-appropriate phrasing can resort to a visual aid and hire an imaginary prompter.

Prompters know all the texts that complete the stage play. Prompters react quickly, discreetly, precisely. The desire for a well-versed prompter is pervasive and non-performance-related. Even experienced and confident tennis players try to catch tips from the distant box via eye contact or quickly try to read the coach's suggestion on the cellphone hidden in the sports bag during the change of ends break, even though it is not allowed.

A Siri or Alexa with a degree in sports psychology coming to the rescue with an app would be great. Whether or not I wish for support is not a question of world-class stature. Rather, it is a basic need for a little support and advice when we feel desperate.

And since not everything external always works or may be forbidden, we need an imaginary adviser. Someone who thinks a prompter couldn't have an adequate sports vocabulary can imagine a coach in that role. The golf caddie that Beckmann and Elbe bring into the game is possibly the perfect imaginary companion.[140]

The adviser in your head

Caddies are true golf experts, usually good players themselves. They are tacticians, advisers, soothers, and choose the clubs. They see the big picture and the details. And as a bonus, they also carry your equipment. It is good to keep a space in your head for such experts. Because then I am able to ask my mind-caddy in any situation where it seems necessary: What is your recommendation?

Daniil Medvedev showed us how effective the mental technique can be when, at the 2022 Australian Open, he was behind by two sets in the quarter-finals against the very powerfully serving Félix Auger-Aliassime and was surprisingly able to turn the match around and win. How did he do it? He didn't quite know what to do.

"I asked myself what Novak would do now."[141] So, Medvedev's inner coach was Novak Djokovic. In a genius move, he picks the number one in the world rankings. And why not? We are free to choose our coach. All of the coaches, psychologists, mothers, fathers, and any experts are at our disposal. And if we want something more modern, we can design our own avatar, available in any situation. Medvedev's inner coach helped him get to the Grand Slam semi-finals.

---

140   Beckmann & Elbe (2008, pg. 75f.).
141   Eurosport (2022).

BELIEVING IN YOURSELF

We become susceptible in a moment of disappointment. It's like the person with a cold who is susceptible to other infections during this phase of weakened immunity. A similar cascade also happens in sports. Lack of success weakens self-confidence. We are at odds with ourselves, with the opponent's luck, and with the referee. And being at odds takes up energy and additional attention, leading us further away from winning a game instead of making a comeback.

As part of their motivational problem situations Kleinert and Sulprizio also describe the mental profile of *wanting to, but not daring to*.[142] They list the causes as lack of **self-confidence**, lack of experience, or negative experiences. The focus should be shifted in the opposite direction to positive things from the past.

- What went well?

- Why did it go well?

- How did that feel?

It is worth taking a deep dive into the events, to recount them, and relive them. These thoughts become snapshots in a short film, a video clip of my success. I then play that film in front of my mind's eye, over and over. This helps me get my thoughts in order, to consciously neglect the negative examples while bringing the positive moments to the fore.

Setting a **somatic marker**[143] can also be beneficial. For instance, by clenching a fist during a successful situation, I anchor this connection between positive mental associations and muscular impulses. This feeling of success can be triggered again later, independent of the actual experience, by clenching the fist. It's a good impulse, for example, at a moment of shaky self-confidence.

---

142   Kleinert & Sulprizio (2019, pg. 173f.).
143   Damasio (1994).

Seeing performance athletes as members of two groups helps us understand the states of self-confidence: those **motivated by success** and those **motivated by failure**. Those motivated by success are true masters at distorting causalities. While they attribute success to themselves, failures tend to be attributed to external factors they are unable to control, such as weather or simply bad luck.

By contrast, those motivated by failure think their success is due to fortunate circumstances and attribute failure to a lack of talent. People who think like this are hardly able to escape the negative spiral, always anticipate success, and start to avoid performance situations and, ultimately, competitions. Those motivated by failure begin to ruminate, their thoughts trapped in the past.

Rumination sets in, always thinking about what went wrong and brooding over one's own mistakes. We feel dejected and helpless.[144] Worst-case scenario, this leads to the athlete dropping out of the sport altogether, or even sports in general, in spite of the affected athletes having once been at the same level as those motivated by success with respect to their abilities and skills.

Allowing yourself secret trials

Failure motivation must be handled carefully. Fear of unpredictable performance requirements and potential embarrassment must be considered. Beckmann and Elbe recommend first trying out training content alone and avoiding comparison to others initially.[145] This allows the performance to take place in a non-competitive space where the athlete can be encouraged and can develop.

The requirement level should be chosen based on the **optimal fit** principal so "the abilities threshold is met." In a work environment, this approach should generally be granted to people who feel pressure when observed and begin to suffer under pressure.

---

144   Stangl (2022).
145   Beckmann & Elbe (2008, pg. 70f).

They must be allowed to gather experiences in protected spaces and develop the corresponding self-image.

So, competition can deter failure-oriented people. Of course, insulating the affected individual is a measure with limited reach. A new understanding of competition must develop sooner or later, geared to success-oriented individuals who experience their competition as stimulating.

Unfortunately, I learned only late in my career to use my competitors' performance as an incentive for myself and learn from other players who are better than I am. Because the many lessons our opponents teach us are basic. They show us our weaknesses, the aspects of our ability that still need work. To truly grow and bring our best, we need strong competitors who push us to the limit.

Viewing your competitor not as the opponent but as a teammate undergoing her own growth process helps us to never lose respect for her. It's a fine line on the court. On the one hand, having irrepressible tenacity is indispensable, not wanting to accept down to the last point that the opponent might be better than you. To push back with all your might against a possible loss. But on the other hand, also being able to acknowledge that the opponent was simply better, either over the course of the game or after a converted break point is essential.

But let's switch once more from the post-match perspective to during-the-match conviction. Belief in the inspired phrase that hope dies last is far more than a cliché. The reality is constant proof.

US Open 1983, second qualifying round. US players Barbie Bramblett and Ann Hulbert are facing off against each other. Bramblett was down 0:6, 0:5, and 0:40.

WILD CARD

The eighteen-year-old believed in herself and defended an incredible eighteen match balls, came back, and won the match. Even if this example isn't the norm, it does show that it's possible to turn around even seemingly impossible situations. The question of whether something is theoretically possible should be the sole decisive factor for believing.

But sometimes we have to endure longer than just a match. Sometimes we have to be patient for the duration of our career. The Taiwanese player Hsieh Su-wei was thirty-five before she was able to reach a Grand Slam quarter final. It happened in 2021 at the Australian Open. It had taken her roughly twenty years from when she first tried to qualify for one of the four major tournaments.

A really good match developed quickly against Johanna Konta, all of the games were close. A single break cost me the first set. Deficit. But I knew I was on it, kept trusting in my game, and made a strong comeback in the second set and won 7:5.

My physical and mental levels were high, and I largely played the best tennis I could muster. Suddenly I was down 0:3 during the third set. I had fought so hard to stay in the game in the second set and to stand my ground against this player, who just wasn't my cup of tea. I had given it all, often successfully, and now, suddenly, the match seemed to slip through my fingers because of one ridiculous inattentive service.

The score was hopeless. I was disappointed and saw the loss coming. Suddenly everything descended on me. I could feel the damn cold and the fatigue from the tough two and a half sets, even more so from the entire day, all the waiting, the tension. I had given it my all, had played a really good match, maybe even my best. Better than many in Stuttgart.

But no one was watching here, no one pushing me to win, no camera showing the replay after a sensational point or how I clenched my fist. I got the deep feeling that everything was too much. Too much adversity all at once. Rarely in my career was I so close to throwing in the internal towel before the final point had been played.

I no longer believed I could win because you just don't win against the number seven in the world after two breaks and 0:3 in the third set. My thoughts began to circle. I mentally went through all of the motivational quotes I had heard on this subject but the essence of which I might not have really understood until this point in my career.

Then came my resolution. A tiny part of me knew that there's at least a theoretical chance. I didn't want to give up. So, I kept playing and kept fighting. I played every point like it was the last of my career. I looked neither back nor forward. I simply stuck to my determination of never giving up. In the end I won 6:3.

When I packed my bag on the court, wrapped myself in several towels to stop freezing, and walked toward the exit, I noticed pride welling up inside of me. I had conquered my weaker self, that crafty loser.

As I exited, I fell into my boyfriend's arms, tired, exhausted, totally depleted but incredibly happy. "That was one of the best wins of my career and no one will ever know that." He just nodded. I had just defeated myself in a positive sense. It is a win I will never forget.

A tennis match lasts until the final point has been played. It can take time. Television stations like to complain because they are unable to plan their programming due to such incalculable factors. The tennis match between John Isner and Nicolas Mahut at Wimbledon 2010 took eleven hours and five minutes and broke all records. Due to rain, this record match took three days to complete. Its start was very ordinary, with

6:4 and 3:6, then two tiebreaks followed, 6:7, 7:6, the harbingers of an incredibly even fifth set. John Isner won the match in the last set with a basketball score of 70:68.

And one more time, because it cannot be emphasized enough: a tennis match lasts exactly until the final point has been played. And that is how long a player has justified reason to believe in themselves, their abilities, and skills, reflected in the **perceived self-efficacy**.

Believing in the "momentum"—which is discussed by live commentators in an inflationary or sometimes somewhat cheeky manner—does give justifiable hope. This is verified by a study in volleyball that showed that successful shots more often result in *more* successful shots, a phenomenon called **hot hand**. The same applies to missed shots.[146]

© picture alliance, Justin Lane, dpa

A fair handshake after every match, regardless of who ultimately had the momentum.

---

146   Raab, Gula & Gigerenzer (2012, pg. 81–94).

SUMMARY

Accepting point deficits, deriding them, or ideally setting them on fire. There are different approaches for overcoming the threat of point deficits.

DEFYING ADVERSITIES

Differentiating between acceptance and proactive change ✳✳✳ resilience creates self-confidence ✳✳✳ accepting the form of the day ✳✳✳ seeing the match as a blank page ✳✳✳ seeing the challenge in the unexpected.

SOFTENING PRESSURE

Nothing goes without pressure ✳✳✳ keeping control of your time ✳✳✳ practicing singularity ✳✳✳ Differentiating the expectations of spectators ✳✳✳ seeing pressure as a privilege.

PROCESSING MISTAKES AND FAILURE

Quickly releasing negative emotions ✳✳✳ righting the psyche via the body ✳✳✳ practicing body language ✳✳✳ forgiving yourself.

CONSTRUCTIVE MIND GAMES

Using mental clips to optimize movements ✳✳✳ focusing on the next moment ✳✳✳ being able to shift the perception from internal to external and from narrow to broad ✳✳✳ stopping your thoughts.

SELF-TALK

Creating action-oriented I-messages ✳✳✳ changing language from negative to positive ✳✳✳ boosting perceived self-efficacy ✳✳✳ establishing the inner prompter.

BELIEVING IN YOURSELF

Focusing on what has worked well ✳✳✳ finding the ideal fit within the scope of your own abilities ✳✳✳ competition as incentive ✳✳✳ believing in yourself until the end.

4

Scoring the big points

©jimmie48 Photography

MATCH POINT: BEING READY AT THE CRITICAL MOMENT

Wanting something so badly. Like a child who is finally allowed to come into the room where the Christmas tree stands with all the tantalizing gifts spread out under it. Like an adult finally starting his vacation after months of working.

Or like all of us after a day when we didn't eat much and are therefore ravenously hungry, our sense of smell is set on super sensitive, and we're about to lose control as the smell of pizza or grilled steak, sauteed shrimp or grilled fish on a stick, or freshly baked bread or croissants hits our nose.

From there the molecules zip up into the square-inch-sized chimney-like olfactory epithelium, which forwards the delightful information to the central nervous system. There the decision is made of whether to directly commandeer the neighbor's grill or try to make it to your own kitchen.

We must really want a win. Being hungry. Blocking out the outside world. Putting the goal and the associated moment ahead of everything else.

ONCE AND NEVER AGAIN

Sometimes in life we have only *one* chance to satisfy that hunger. This can be true for Olympic participants. Since the Games only happen every four years and top athletic performance isn't guaranteed to be permanent, many years of training can come down to a single Olympic appearance. One must be prepared for this singularity that focuses all the pressure in the world on this one competition. The start signal comes and we have to function.

"We know that we have only *one* chance," said President of the EU Commission Ursula von der Leyen in 2021, prior to the world climate conference in Glasgow, Scotland, referring to the limited amount of time remaining to, for instance, reduce emissions.[147] "We have just one chance to do a demolition," said Peter Bodes, head of the bomb disposal team, meaning the latent threat to and the responsibility for his team and their families.[148] "And some have only *one* chance in life to make it to the Olympic Games," commented Max Rendschmidt, who won two gold medals in kayaking at the 2016 Olympics and spoke out against canceling the Games[149] when there was talk about canceling the Tokyo Games due to the Covid-19 pandemic.

That one chance where everything comes to a head happens often. It is a form of singularity, something special life has to offer. At least in sports we want to be well prepared for this exclusive moment. That is why we should practice it. The right methodology has existed for a long time and it has a name that makes it easy to relate: **singularity training**.

In doing so, the athlete is asked to perform a one-time task. He or she must implement something for with only one attempt. The pressure of the moment is critical and must be kept up, and can even be increased by, for instance, having the team stand around the individual in a semi-circle. Some type of punishment can also be imposed if the task is not completed.

Such a singularity occurred on May 19, 2012, and it involved several players at once. FC Bayern Munich was playing FC Chelsea in the Champions League final. After ninety minutes the score was 1:1. The game went into extra time during which Bayern Munich player Arjen Robben missed a penalty kick. A first wink? The game remained tied and had to be decided via penalty kicks.

And then what happened no one would have thought possible. Several players refused their service to Coach Jupp Heynckes and did not want to take the decisive penalty kicks. Too much pressure, too much responsibility, and just too much unrepeatable singularity!

147   Tagesschau (2021).
148   German Insurance Association (2018).
149   Rendschmidt & Friebe (2020).

© picture alliance, Daniel Karmann, dpa

The decisive moment: Staying calm and setting the pace within the limits of one's abilities.

The situation was new. Even though Bayern Munich had played this final just two years before (back then against Inter Milan), several players had participated in both finals, but a penalty shootout has a very different feel and, in particular, a very different kind of pressure. Every shot has to go in. Of course, the opponent's strike rate also matters. Everything is at stake, that is to say, the European soccer throne.

Moreover, this final is taking place in front of the home crowd, right in Munich, in a sold-out stadium. If that isn't singularity! The game's drama also contributed to the intensification. Bayern Munich had outplayed the opponent with a corner ratio of 20:1 and an odds ratio of 7:3. They simply had to win the penalty shootout.

Or was Robben's missed penalty kick in extra time a bad omen? Some of the players may have thought so since they were not in the right mental state to be able to take on the necessary responsibility. They lacked faith in their self-efficacy.

René Paasch, Professor of Sports Psychology and Life Coaching, also recognized the deficit. "Pro soccer players tend to give the impression that they possess a lot of dispositional self-confidence. But when their team has to play a penalty shootout at an important championship game their self-confidence can suddenly head south."[150]

From there Bayern now had to accept Chelsea's win of the penalty shootout. Several players could not cope with the impact of singularity, possibly because they had not practiced it before. All of them almost certainly had sufficient reason to trust in their penalty-kicking skills. All of them had taken an endless number of penalty shots into the back of the net. But being champions during training is a long way from being tournament champions because, except for the distance, the random practice penalty shot doesn't have much in common with the special Champions League final penalty kick.

---

150   Paasch (2015)

Eberspächer lists what every Bayern player would have needed to engage in a singular situation with the expectation of succeeding:[151]

- Unforced conviction of his own abilities and skills;

- Appropriate assessment of the requirements;

- Confidence in his ability to bring the necessary performance at that moment; and

- The ability to tap into the optimal motion sequence even if it is required in a difficult situation.

According to Eberspächer it is not just singularity that must be practiced. Athletes must also be familiar with the competition-typical thought process of predicting their results. **Prediction training** ties in with previously themed goal-setting, but now in reference to a training session.

The power of the own assessment

Keeping with the example of the soccer penalty kick, the player is asked to take five penalty kicks. But first, he will predict how many of the shots will reach their mark. The effect can be amplified by making the prediction in front of the teammates who are watching. The situation becomes even more intense if a punishment is agreed upon for not reaching the predicted quota. Another way to intensify the exercise would be to have the player specify where he plans to place the ball prior to taking the shot, without the goalie's knowledge of course.

All of these things prepare a pressure-laden competitive situation where this type of situational goal-setting is also undertaken.

The next step in singularity training is sharpening awareness of the fact that in a competition there is often just that one chance that must be used without compromise and without distraction.

---

151   Eberspächer (2012).

The feeling that is triggered by such a singular situation must not be unfamiliar and thus is initiated again and again during training. But—and this is important—only once per training session.

For instance, the coach might tell the player fifteen minutes before the end of practice that he must still complete one last task: to take the final and only penalty kick that will determine whether that player will leave practice satisfied or dissatisfied.

The effect can be amplified by accessing the player's imagination: Imagine it is not the end of the practice session but the end of a soccer game. Ninetieth minute, 0:0, the goal decides the game. Or the end of a penalty shootout, *the* penalty shootout of the Champions League final. Your shot decides. The closer the thoughts can be brought to a real situation, the better.

And the more similar the acoustic and optical impressions are to a real situation, the more effective. Why not use the stadium for realistic experiences, particularly before an impending home game? In this special training situation, the spectator noise would have to be provided by the stadium's speaker system. Everything else can be imitated: who stands where and when, who goes where and when, even the floodlights can be replicated.

At the Bayern versus Chelsea final, the players stood united at the centerline. From the perspective of the penalty taker: I am the only one who had to leave that familiar circle of team and colleagues to go the approximate forty meters to the penalty spot, by myself. A total of 62,500 spectators to the left, the right, and in front of me, and yet it was completely quiet. Thirty seconds to think about the singularity of my shot and how the home crowd will celebrate me when I score.

And beyond that, how the fans will suffer if I miss. The latter would be the wrong prediction, the wrong target option, the wrong connection to singularity that happens primarily if I do not practice it. Chelsea won the penalty shootout 4:3 and, with that, also from a sports psychology perspective, a historic game.

Some situations in life put pressure on us. To be able to successfully or at least better master them, we should approximate them with the appropriate practice and training. Moreover, we should be familiar with a strategy often described by experts that has helped many to stay calm: implementing routines and rituals. They can verifiably help us regulate our activation level and block out interfering factors at the moment when tension is highest.

MAINTAINING ROUTINES AND RITUALS

Those looking for insight into rituals best look beyond western borders and western world views to where rituals conform to traditional beliefs—for instance, Japan. The behavior of the Japanese tells us much about their relationship with life, their teachers, and with themselves.

Let's take the routine of the ink painter. It includes testing the brushes, thoughtful preparation, careful grinding of the ink, positioning the paper, and pausing before starting. All of this has "such expressive power that it feels like a picture to the viewer," writes Eugen Herrigel in his notes.[152]

The master ink painter, the master flower arranger, the master archer—all follow a pattern that serves internal composure while simultaneously detaching from external influences. Beckmann and Elbe emphasize that rituals are "somewhat ceremonial and can contain superstitious elements."[153]

One always leaves the locker room first, the other one always comes onto the field. The clothing must always be the same, regardless of its condition. Genuflecting and turning the eyes up to heaven before the game is a **ritual**. The gold chain talisman, the sweatband are good luck charms, always.

---

152 Herrigel (2011, pg. 52 et seq.).
153 Beckmann & Elbe (2008, pg. 87).

Superstition also caused the former national soccer coach Berti Vogts to choose monotone clothing when he was a defender for the team Borussia Mönchengladbach in the 1970s. "I always wore the same white socks, as least as long as we won."[154]

The former Yugoslavian national soccer coach Miroslav Stević said before the 1998 World Championships that he always wore the same t-shirt, and if his team lost, he immediately threw it away. Completely different if they won: "When everything goes well, I'm afraid to change the slightest thing. Even the toothpaste."[155]

The magic of the fine thread

This might make us smile, but we quickly go from shaking our head to nodding when we recall our own experiences with clothing. Do we not feel like two different people when we wear a suit or evening gown as opposed to casual athletic wear or tough work clothes? Some who always wear jeans feel like they are in costume when they are suddenly out in public in a tuxedo. And it has nothing to do with the texture of the material or the cut.

Rather, it is about the visual impression I make in my hometown mirror and the effect I consequently anticipate when I step outside the door. Clothing and psyche in an invisible dialogue, isn't it absurd? But it's true.

Let us indulge ourselves in a brief look at the children. They act intuitively and mentally beneficial when they put on a Barca, Real, or Inter jersey before soccer practice. Because won't they now run a little bit faster on the pitch, inspired by the feeling of being one of the big ones? Won't they put a little more spin on the tennis ball with the logo of Roger Federer or Rafael Nadal on their shirt?

---

154   Brunner (1998).
155   Ibidem.

Rafael Nadal is also influential in another way as he is probably the most notable representative of the ritual. He pulls the seat of his pants with his fingertips, then his shirt at the left shoulder, the right shoulder, he rubs the bridge of his nose, pushes his hair back over his left ear, briefly goes back to the bridge of his nose, then pushes his hair back over his right ear. It's always the same. The sequences can be layered like copies.

People never grow tired of poking fun, but given the Spaniard's supremacy, they should be better able to differentiate silly tricks from effective tricks by now. At least Nadal's opponents stopped laughing years ago.

Rituals offer support in life, in general. It is most obvious when the ritual is interrupted. How about when the daily newspaper isn't on the breakfast table? We like repetition because we can rely on it. It always repeats itself, at the same place, at the same time. It makes us feel secure.

For some, the morning coffee is the necessary flywheel to get the day off to a good start. Others like the familiar smell of freshly ground coffee beans, and others like the ritual of putting the filter in the machine or simply pressing the button.

Familiarity creates security

Someone who has been the driver for years and suddenly, for whatever reason, is relegated to being the passenger feels out of place. He feels insecure because he had to leave his familiar terrain and because he had to give up control of the vehicle.

These insights help us understand the power of **routines**. They give us reliability and protection, all the way back to the beginning of our life in the form of bedtime rituals. The hug, the goodnight kiss, the stuffed animal on the right. We already need this at a young age; rituals provide a framework, they "provide contexts within a child's life."[156]

---

156   Morgenthaler & Hauri (2010).

And routines help keep us from getting distracted, which helps prevent our thoughts from wandering and pays off in every challenging situation. Because the threat of distraction lurks in every moment, it isn't linked to a specific task.

To avoid losing focus, Rafael Nadal links several rituals. He follows a pattern when he walks along the lines of the court without touching them, when he always hangs his towel over the advertising board in the same way, and when he positions the bottles in front of him during the change of ends, aligning them identically, one cold the other one lukewarm.

His rituals are not snapshots but recurring productions. Completely structured, they give his game a foundation, support, familiarity.

From this we deduce that we should not wait for rituals and routines to find us. Rather, we must make them our own. One moment that requires particular care, in sports as well as anywhere else, is the moment before the start. The spectators cannot capture my attention. And I also cannot think about my private life, about bad performances, or the next vacation. And since thoughts are famously free, we must reign them in.

I can do so with rituals or routines respectively. To differentiate: the previously discussed rituals usually don't contain goal-oriented physiological elements; therefore, they take place independently of the impending specific movement task. Furthermore, they also permit superstitious tendencies.

By contrast, routines include "skills that help complete the impending task" and have the goal of "optimizing action preparation."[157] It is about running through forms of movement that partially or completely anticipate the impending task.

---

157   Beckmann & Elbe (2008, pg. 87).

WILD CARD

The athlete must consciously create a framework that begins ideally with the focus on breathing and ends immediately prior to the actual action. This creates a good foundation for an unimpeded concentration phase.

It is important to me to take the time between points during a match to process the previous point, to collect myself and plan my next move. But all of that has to happen within twenty-five seconds, because that is all the time players have between rallies in tennis.

*In the past, that time measurement was just a rule of thumb that a referee would only penalize in cases of severe, regular violation. Since the 2018 US Open, a clock in the corner of the court, the **shot clock**, counts down the time. It is activated by the referee as soon as a rally ends.*

Therefore, we know when the next point must begin and penalties come into effect immediately. Even just a one- or two-second delay triggers a warning, and the second violation already results in a point deduction.

So that it is possible to run through these three steps—processing, calming down, planning—in such a short period of time, I have created an always similar routine for myself: after the point, I go to my towel and briefly mentally grade the previous point:

* *Was everything tactically correct?*
* *What can I do better?*

Then I take a deep breath and, for a moment, try to not think about anything and just relax. I am able to do so by "retreating" to a corner of the court where I "feel safe" and can focus on one part of my body, for instance, my breathing. Or consciously dropping my shoulders, which are tense from stress, with each exhalation.

It seems easier to relax if you can find a spot somewhere on the periphery that is less visible, where you can therefore feel more protected for this moment of inner peace. By taking a few slow, deep breaths, I try to come down mentally and physically. It often helps if I close my eyes.

After a few seconds rest, I turn around and the activation phase begins. I make a few faster movements, a few quick taps and side-steps, something that gives me renewed energy. It can also be encouraging inner self-talk, such as "Let's go!" Then I have the ball kids give me the balls, and I choose very specific ones for the next point.

At this point my specific choices will remain my little secret. I think it's very important to create private partial aspects within these routines and rituals that no one else if privy to. A system we have customized for ourselves and that enables us to be "fully present" in the blink of an eye. The more individual and thus authentic, the better.

Routines and superstition live very close together here and are wonderfully combinable. Linking objectively nonfunctional aspects with functional ones is not reprehensible as long as it feels better. This activation phase has been rehearsed and studied a million times and has thus been automated.

So now my head is clear, allowing me to plan my next move. And when I step up to the line for the serve, I bounce the ball in my own way. This gives me the necessary composure and the rhythm for my serving motion during this final segment of this break between points, and it also relaxes me because I have always done it this way on all the courts around the world.

Olympic shooter Barbara Engleder also knows the power of a routine before a competition. "I take the weapon off the stand and position it against my shoulder. Before I focus on the target, I look over the top of the gun and check two points: my shoulder and my support arm. And if

I get a bad feeling as I do so, I immediately abort the shot and start over." A new attempt, build up composure and self-confidence, using the routine as a vehicle.

Golfers are very adept at routines—other than the fact that it is a way for them to consolidate their attention—that allow them to prepare and complete their shots. Disruptive thoughts no longer have a place in an optimized period of time during which pre-shot routine, shot and post-shot routine succeed each other without interruption. Nothing should be able to happen to a shot that is embedded in structured buffer actions.

Sports psychologist Jürgen Beckmann wrote a detailed example of a pre-shot routine in golf: tee up the ball, take three steps behind the ball, check the wind, make a decision regarding club and shot, look at the target, look at the ball, visualize, two test swings, go to the ball, "address" the ball, two waggles, tense up, and relax and go.[158]

The pre-shot routine of the world-famous golfer Jack Nicklaus is said to have a cinematic quality—a short movie in which, in his mind's eye, he sees the ball after playing the shot, flying, landing, rolling, and dropping into the hole.[159]

Bernhard Langer also explains how he resorts to the "pre-shot" routine he has developed over time, which is thought out down to the second. It takes precisely forty-two seconds. This routine is important for over-coming the, in golf jargon, "yips"—uncontrolled muscle twitching in the forearm—and to take a very precise shot.

"When I pull my club out of the bag, I take two trial swings. Then I step up to the ball, look for my target, take aim with my club, make two or three corrections in my posture and swing."[160]

Tiger Woods, arguably the most well-known and most successful golfer on the circuit, used an uncomplicated and brief routine.

---

158 Beckmann (2015, pg. 52).
159 Ibidem.
160 Bogner (no year).

SCORING THE BIG POINTS

To get a sense of rhythm for the subsequent shot, he takes several or fewer trial swings, depending on the situation. These are controlled and slow, while he concentrates largely on his balance.

He then visualizes his target in the distance, for instance a flag or a tree, and then a target in his immediate vicinity that might be right in front of the ball. The closer target, which is an extension of the other one, can help with alignment or rather aiming. Once he feels good while standing over the ball, he takes his shot.

At this point we will briefly digress to decision-making and the necessary consequence that should go hand in hand with it. In 1987, Heinz Heckhausen and Peter Gollwitzer developed the **Rubicon model**,[161] an action model that fixes the forming of an intention as the moment in which we cross the river Rubicon like Cesar and can longer turn back.

Adhering to our decision

Once a decision has been made at a certain threshold, it must be seen through. Sports psychologist Jürgen Beckmann calls it "crossing the line of commitment."[162]

He considers the golf routine as a vivid example. There is an imaginary line on the ground on the short path between the trial swing and the actual shot. Once we have crossed it, our decision for the club and type of shot becomes law. We deny ourself any parallel thoughts. Hence, we must be above any doubt, meaning: we must completely accept the decision.

However, that's not enough if we want to develop into a top athlete. Let us push the limits further: we will therefore hang our mental agreement with the decision a little higher. It is like the high-jump bar that is raised

---

161 Heckhausen, Gollwitzer & Weinert (1987).
162 Beckmann (2015, pg. 54).

inch by inch because we consider ourselves capable of further surpassing ourselves. So, we don't just settle for acceptance but embrace the decision starting now and truly like it. And even this liking leaves more room for higher bars.

- But what do we want more than liking our decision?

- What would be an argument against simply being enthusiastic about our own actions for which there are no longer any alternatives at this point?

- Would that not be the deluxe feeling of satisfaction and therefore self-confidence and motivation?

The decision over how high the bar must hang is very personal. What is clear is that the more we become one with our decision, the wider the door opens to a great performance.

Taking advantage of the effect of routines is not a question of the athlete's age but a more general one. The sports psychologist Dr. Kai Engbert has written a mental training manual specifically for children and adolescents. He considers components of mental training to be beneficial as early as ages ten to thirteen.[163]

That seems quite early. But only if you think that a ten-year-old would be on the couch having an animated conversation with a psychologist about traumatic experiences as a young child. Of course, that scenario doesn't exist. Mental health topics are usually not discussed in a one-on-one setting at that age but rather with the entire team or at least in small groups.

And here, it is also less about working on accrued problems and more about looking at the sport, completely unstressed. Together, the child with the team can search for moments that cannot be managed with just strength, endurance, and speed but also require mental work. It is literally an opportunity to create awareness at a young age that the mind has just as much right to receive training as the body. And not just the right, but the necessity.

---

163   Engbert (2017, pg. 10).

The advantage of early intervention is obvious. It enables the athletes to manage small challenges more easily and in a playful way. It generates pride, self-confidence, and prepares them for a more advanced level. And it reduces the drop-out rate—the number of athletes who leave the sport early.[164]

MY ROUTINES ON THE GOLF COURSE

Before every shot:
- Assess the ball position.
- Check the wind/height difference.
- Measure the distance, calculate/estimate the expected distance.
- Become aware of potential obstacles and dangers.
- Choose the club, two to three trial swings on the ball to get a sense of the site (grass, sand, slope, etc.).
- Move behind the ball (in extension of the target, visualize the trajectory and the shot).
- Some more practice swings to build up a feel for the shot.
- As soon as I feel comfortable, I approach the ball while simultaneously entering a "zone" in which I only think about the execution.
- Stand at the ball and shift from one foot to the other to get the right stance.
- Look at the ball and the target three times.
- I initiate my subsequent swing and shot by turning my head slightly to the right.

Before every putt:
- Right before the putt, I slightly pull first on my right pant leg and then the left.
- I read the break first from behind the hole, then from the side.

Fig. 2: Routine of German national league golfer Pablo Brunner

---

164   Engbert (2017, pg. 11).

Mental literacy can be built year by year. By the time children are old enough to be on a squad, there should also be room for talking about routines and integrating them into the sport, as the routine of the then seventeen-year-old golfer Pablo Brunner, German national league player and member of the state team, shows (see fig. 2).

Mentally collecting yourself

Something that is very complex in golf, because this sport requires a special kind of concentration and precision, can also be applied to many other sports in a small way: the routine before the seven-meter-throw in handball, the penalty shot in ice hockey or soccer, before the gymnastics freestyle program, the pole vault, or the ski-cross race. All competitions require us to mentally collect ourselves, to build up self-confidence, block out interfering factors, focus on our breath, and prepare for the impending action with a visualization based on positive anticipation.

Competitors outside of sports can also benefit. Whether it is a negotiation, a moderation, or vocal presentation, all situations can be preceded by visualization, which is inserted like a routine just before the event. It must, of course, be related to reality.

For instance, fantasizing about everyone hugging and singing happy songs after an upcoming job interview will never be anything more than a fantasy. However, my visualization of myself as a likable and quick-witted applicant could become real.

For some athletes, the match-day routine begins in the morning when they get up. Everything has to be in its place and everything must proceed as usual: the same breakfast, the same match outfit, the same practice court for the warm-up, the same, the same, the same. And, ultimately, all elite athletes have some type of functional routine of things that must be done *just so* to provide assurance.

Sample routines

- **Morning routines:** *Doing something that is always feasible, regardless of how you feel or where you are. It can be a short walk, a meditation or some exercises or yoga poses in your bedroom or hotel room.*

- **Pre-performance routines:** *A warm-up for the actual performance, a preparation of the essentials, also not location-dependent. For instance, music, a particular song you frequently listen to before a performance, or briefly retreating to a quiet place and, by yourself or with a partner, going over what you plan to do today.*

- **During-performance routines:** *Specify processes for breaks and other time gaps during the performance. For example, in tennis: walking to the towel before an important point, or the previously determined chronology of what you will eat and drink during the change of sides. It could be a deep breath before the critical grip or closing your eyes to visualize an intended technique.*

- **Reset routines:** *When something didn't go so well, create a routine that allows you to reset to zero and start over. In tennis: after a series of lost games, wrap new grip tape on the racket handle and change sweatbands; after losing a set, put on a new outfit during a bathroom break, and consciously choose a different color. Outside of sports: take a drink of water, take a quick break, look out the window, and mentally leave the room for a few seconds. Then refocus.*

- **Flow-routine:** *This is not about developing a new process but—if things go well—merely holding on to functioning processes. Letting specific ideas get quieter, turning off the mind and allowing the automated movement patterns to unwind on their own. "Never change a working system" applies to big things and little things.*

Automating routines for the competition

This chance of more security alone practically pushes us to develop suitable routines, to deliberately practice them, and internalize them. Because only then, under pressure of time in a match, in front of spectators when everything is at stake, can they help us increase our focus and restore the necessary calm.

And what happens when we are unable to implement the routine in the usual manner? It cannot throw the top performer off course; he still has to be able to function. According to Eberspächer, "top performers and key players are able to regulate their appraisal in a way that allows them to still succeed even when they are confronted with major demands outside of the routine."[165]

Focusing before the return: using routines for better preparation.

---

165   Eberspächer (2011, pg. 50).

SUMMARY

In order to remain focused and concentrate in singular situations, singularity must be trained. While it is not possible to conjure identical scenarios with the identical emotional state, approximations are possible and absolutely recommended. Furthermore, rituals and routines pave the way to a feeling of overall security and familiarity.

ONCE AND NEVER AGAIN

Putting yourself in situations where you allow yourself only one attempt *** Increasing pressure by creating a competition-like atmosphere *** Increasing pressure by predicting the result *** Being sure of yourself and familiar with the requirements.

CULTIVATING ROUTINES AND RITUALS

Rituals: give us assurance and support *** Routines: developing and running through movement patterns that anticipate parts or all of an impending task or prepare for it *** personalized sequence *** help to mentally collect yourself and build self-confidence *** different conceivable timeframes *** the more personal, the better *** follow your gut.

5

Personal development

© picture alliance, David Crosling, dpa

GAME, SET, MATCH: DESIGNING CAREERS

Often fractions of seconds decide the outcome. It is so tight that a finish photo or calibrated lines on software have to be consulted to make a fair decision. It would be presumptuous to speak of a difference in performance. And like seconds, sometimes hours, or entire days can be the deciding factor, or sometimes it is the form of the day. And often it is an entire season that counts and grants the athlete a few extra tenths or a botched-up day.

After the first half of the campaign during the 2014/15 season, Borussia Dortmund, a top team in the Bundesliga, was in second-to-last place—a relegation spot. The second league already had its teeth in the Dortmund team. But at the end of the season, the Borussians were in respectable seventh place and thus were able to play for a spot in the Europa League. Sometimes it's the teeny-tiny time frames, but sometimes also many months that decide success and failure.

And then there is the really big picture: the years-long timeline of an entire career. Which performance and competition highlights does one aspire to or may have already reached?

The Australian tennis player Ashleigh Barty was twenty-five years old when she chose an unusually early retirement because she had reached two of her important career highlights: winning at Wimbledon and Melbourne, among other reasons.

At age fifty-four, the Japanese soccer player Kazuyoshi Miura is still not thinking about quitting. He is considered the world's oldest professional in his sport. Let's break this down to one simple question: what do elite athletes want?

PROMISING SUCCESS

Is success just a social trap that the high-performance individual continues to step into? It is worth considering why society continuously lays its inhumane demand traps without considering the magnitude of its actions.

Why do people appreciate major league sports more than the minor leagues, the Olympics more than the Paralympics? Because, as the Olympic slogan suggests, they want faster, higher, and further. Only when the pole vaulter clears the six-meter mark, is the spectators' need for the spectacular met.

The media tirelessly makes projections about, for instance, the status of Grand Slam wins of tennis players or the official game goal record of soccer players. In the headlines, the quantity of goals has replaced the quality, likely because the longing for record-breaking news is more easily placated with a big number rather than with over-embellished statements about elegance.

- But what about the athlete who trained for weeks, months, years with dedication, and on the crucial day doesn't perform and falls short of his capabilities?

- Will he, too, be valued, honored, even noticed?

Decision day turns into Judgment Day. Those who serve the spectators and do not even get on the podium are overlooked. More critical but quite fittingly: the player is ignored.

The fans' view of sports is binary and thus simple. Someone is either successful or not. And that is how society educates the athlete who is focused on winning and nothing but winning. "You measure everything by success," summarizes 235-time national handball team player Henning Fritz. "There is only black and white."

But, of course, there is more than winning and losing, more than the final, the conclusive showdown. The real insight into life in performance sports is often given short shrift. Says Fritz: "It is important to incorporate the experiences in elite sports into society."

Being successful largely means being able to ignore or overcome the weight of expectations. Many are crushed by that pressure. Just because we only hear about a few cases doesn't mean that the number of those affected is, in fact, low.

Feeling overwhelmed is one thing, but publicly admitting it to yourself and the world is something else entirely. The dedicated search for success might also lead to an unsatisfactory, endless path. Because one nasty aspect of success is that it takes a long time for it to appear.

The Professor of Economic Science Wolfgang Vieweg says: "Success seems to find its own path, even around lots of corners. It is about finding viable, possible paths."[166]

What is success? That's not an easy question.

- *Are we successful if we have a big house and drive a fancy car?*
- *Or if we operate a business, have employees?*
- *Or if we simply do what we truly love?*
- *Or something entirely different: is success being modest and therefore satisfied with the bare necessities?*

Many will choose wealth and social status. But in my opinion, it's not that simple.

It is, of course, in the eye of the beholder. Answers will vary depending on society, age, and life context: the thirteen-year-old who got an A in math, the twenty-two-year-old who finds his life companion, the thirty-year-old who wins Olympic gold, and the forty-two-year-old who gets the advertised job. By saying success is exploiting opportunities,[167] Vieweg creates a universally applicable basis.

---

166 Vieweg (2015, pg. 4).
167 Ibidem (2015, pg. 4).

To me, success is never standing still. To continue to evolve, to continue to get to know yourself better and improve in what you do. How we handle ourselves, be it professionally, on the path to personal goals, or simply as a human being and in how we engage with others. To me, this includes never stopping learning and always maintaining a certain amount of openness and curiosity, taking something away from others, and applying new discoveries to one's own principals and actions, even if one already possesses a lot of know-how.

It is important to have the freedom to develop your own standards, to recognize your own inner values and remain true to them. I draw inner strength, self-confidence, and a clear path in my life from those things, which leads to success.

To me, success ultimately means the extent of inner contentment, being at peace with yourself because you have created something good from your own abilities, to have provided added value to yourself and others. To have found self-fulfillment. I believe that on the journey to inner success, the outer success shows up on its own.

That is also tennis legend Billie Jean King's view. She values inner success above all else and makes it a prerequisite for happiness, fulfillment, and, finally, outer success. At the same time, she bemoans the lack of integrity and the unfortunate shift of emphasis to the external and material: "Many of the problems we are seeing nowadays concerning a lack of integrity stem from the fact that people are putting the emphasis on 'outer success'—how much we make, how much we own, how we look, etc."[168]

---

168   King (2008, pg. 152).

© picture alliance, Bernd Weißbrod, dpa

Achieving success and relishing the moment.

Success is largely a condition variable that is not solely influenced by the athlete, their training, form of the day, and performance level. It is also influenced by external factors that depend on the conditions of the day, such as wind, temperature, humidity, light, fans, event location, sport, and potentially, one's own teammates.

Success indicators can thus really not be standardized. People are different. Some cramp up in the cold, others cannot tolerate hot conditions.

Hence, identical performances can produce different results, and, in turn, different per Hence, identical formances can have the same results.[169]

For me, developing a holistic perspective was fundamental. To see myself more as a human being in its entirely and not just as a tennis pro. When I was doing well and felt balanced, my body also responded, and I played good tennis.

But as soon as I tried to force performances and goals, I got stuck. We invite success just by continuing to do high-quality work on ourselves. You could say it is up to each of us to accept the invitation.

And it is so important to break away from external evaluations and focus on the self. To create a checklist of the things that really matter.

- What does success mean to me?

- What do I expect from my sport?

- What do I expect from my life?

- Who do I want to be?

"To me it is more important to be a good person than a good tennis player,"[170] said Ashleigh Barty after her Wimbledon win in 2021. It did not sound pretentious, but honest. And it is noteworthy because such quotes are rare.

One of her soulmates is ski racer Linus Straßer. "I have already achieved so much, have made so much progress. And that is what's most important.

169   Güllich & Krüger (2013, pg. 541).
170   Ran (2021).

Not just in sports but also as a human being," he said in an *ARD* interview. He had just placed seventh in the Olympic slalom competition, and he missed a place on the podium by twenty-three hundredths of a second in Peking in February 2022.

So, he wasn't on the podium where he would have been given the ultimate respect. He also said that "he really has nothing to be ashamed of," because "we usually lose more often than we win. That's just part of it." A devastatingly straightforward statement that should be heard.

Benefiting from losses

The topic gains even more steam when we pose the question: what teaches us more, a loss or a win? Aren't there a lot of athletes who fall into a deep hole after a big final win, while many losers draw strength from their loss and train away mistakes with lots of motivation?

Confirmation comes from an authoritative source. US automobile pioneer Henry Ford said that our failures are often more successful than our successes.

Linus Straßer ended his remarks after the Olympic slalom race with a pragmatic statement endowed with basic satisfaction: "That's elite sports, and it's part of it, and ultimately that's what makes it so incredibly beautiful." Flow expert Mihaly Csikszentmihalyi, who once more explains the possibilities of our influence, can add to that: "like luck, success cannot be pursued; it must happen." Namely as "an unintended side-effect, when a person applies himself to a cause that is greater than he."[171]

---

171   Csikszentmihalyi (2017).

> *When we operate in a performance-oriented area, have goals and very high standards, we tend to want to force success. We are impatient and want the shortest and quickest path to our dreams, or we think that if only we work hard enough, we are practically entitled to success.*
>
> *And I must contradict this fallacy, notably from my own bad experience. Because sometimes it's better to be clever. The crux is knowing the difference:*
>
> - *When is it appropriate to be harder on myself?*
> - *And when should I be smart about my actions because I do better when I'm easier on myself?*
>
> *And that can certainly mean training less sometimes or playing in fewer tournaments.*

And, of course, success also has a second phase: the time after the success, or more precisely, the time between the current and the hoped-for next success. Because we quickly realize that the world functions within a merciless category system.

On one side is the singular success that might also have been fortunate because all things instrumental fell into place on that particular day, including luck and happenstance. But only those who are able to rise above the presumption of luck and happenstance and can validate their success and make it one for the history books with a subsequent success will ascend the Olympus of truly determined competitors.

But success number two doesn't make it easier, but likely even harder. First of all, we should definitely relish the deserved exultation after success number one, but also limit it in good time to be able to focus on new tasks. Self-satisfaction must quickly give way to the aspiration to climb the next eight-thousander.

Nobel price recipient in literature Bernard Shaw condenses this idea: "Man can climb to the highest summits, but he cannot dwell there long."[172] And we should realize this: starting now, opponents, who are particularly motivated to keep the current champion from another summit attempt, will stand in the way.

Let us ask the master of extreme mountain climbing Reinhold Messner how to make it to the top reliably. His response: "The less a person depends on success the less likely it is that he will fall."[173] And he clarifies that those who want to force success are more likely to fall, to fail. So, that's the difficult task we must master, to be hungry for success, but not to want to make it happen at all costs.

Creating images of success

It is absolutely legitimate and even advisable to create our success goal early on in our mind by visualizing it. The individual athlete can do so just as well as the team. The appropriate images, ideally very precise and realistic, can be developed together with the sports psychologist. Details matter, such as auditory impressions, the stadium atmosphere—whatever can be brought in for support via loudspeakers during the visualization process. The success video in your head can be used during a practice game already, and can thereby be translated into a match scenario.

And we should be prepared for two sobering reality checks. First of all, there is no advance praise, no bonus. Unfortunately, we do not carry over points from old successes to the new contest. Or at least only rarely. Every tennis tournament, every basketball season, and every marathon starts again at zero. And secondly, not everyone will share in our triumph. "Success can also make you lonely; it creates haters and generates fear," says Lothar Linz.[174]

---

172   Shaw (n. d.).
173   Messner (n. d.).
174   Linz (2014, pg. 174).

SEARCHING FOR MEANING AND FINDING YOUR IDENTITY

Sleeping too many hours on a soft mattress hurts like hell. "I roll onto my side, coughing and groaning, and curl up into the fetal position." Most of the time, he then lies on the floor to avoid the pain. "After three decades of running and stopping, jumping, after countless leaps and hard landings my body no longer feels like it is mine," Andre Agassi sums up in his autobiography.

His body bothered him not just after but during his career, especially his spine with spondylolisthesis and slipped disks.[175]

On the flip side of his work-life balance are more than 100 weeks as number one in the world rankings, eight Grand Slam titles, and a fortune of more than $100 million. But is it really a balance? When considering the physical limitations as a form of injury, Steffi Graf, Andre Agassi's wife, can also be included in the conversation.

In a tweet from February 1, 2014, she wrote: "When you win while injured, your status as a winner of course goes up. But injuries cannot be the price of success."[176] At this point, it can be said that setting off pain against success isn't easy. The currency isn't the same. Bertolt Brecht, not an athlete but a wise man, added: "Major sports begin where they have long stopped being healthy."[177]

After a long injury break in 2021, it was unclear whether Rafael Nadal would be able to return to the ATP tour. He had turned thirty-five in June of that same year, not an unusual time to end a career. But Serena Williams and Roger Federer have disproven any theories about

---

175   Agassi (2009).
176   Graf (2022).
177   Brecht (n. d.).

a biological performance peak in tennis when they competed at Wimbledon at age thirty-nine. Of course, not the prize money, but instead the passion for the sport, the competitive spirit, the record appeal, and the incomparable feeling of recognition are sufficient enticement to try it again and again.

Being closer to the age of the average pensioner than one's schooldays doesn't count. Nadal, too, felt the allure of the ATP tour magic. He played one little preparatory tournament and then stood in the world-famous Rod Laver Stadium and won his twenty-first Grand Slam title at the 2022 Australian Open after a five-hour and twenty-one-minute final. A record.

At the award ceremony he choked up, as he spoke about "one of the most emotional moments" of his career. Does this explain the significance? Overall Nadal won twenty matches in a row in the first quarter. That, too, must have been an indescribable feeling.

It starts with the final steps through the changing room hallways. It is an exciting moment, the walk onto the court. For instance, at the Porsche Grand Prix in 2017, semi-final day, I am playing against Simona Halep. I stand in the stadium catacombs, lots of technicians with headsets are bustling about, camera operators are filming me from the front, the side, the back.

Then a brief interview in front of a sponsor's cardboard wall, streamed live in the stadium where 4,000 people are waiting to see you play and hopefully win. Someone counts down: "3-2-1-go!"

The heavy black curtain is pushed to the side. The fog machines hiss, the entrance music blares, and you hear your name through the loudspeakers. It's staging and drama like before a boxing match. People leap out of their seats and cheer for you.

© Jimmie48 Photography

Spectacular: the sport as a spectator and media event.

"It is a fact that man needs recognition, validation and appreciation,"[178] says the Austrian sport sociologist Ottmar Weiß. Sports with their count-less action areas have created a particularly well-suited stage for humans.

It starts with the basketball net in the driveway, the ping-pong table at the playground, the beach volleyball court at the outdoor pool, and the skatepark behind it. And on to the track and field stadium, the ice-skating rink, the soccer and baseball stadiums. And it ends in Acapulco, where cliff divers plunge into water thirty-five meters below, and in Nazaré, Portugal, where daring surfers ride twenty-meter waves.

---

178   Weiß (1999).

WILD CARD

The German surfer Sebastian Steudtner won the Big Wave award—the equivalent of a World Championship—there in 2010, 2015, and 2020. And that takes care of it all: lots of recognition and lots of appreciation. Every witness and fan of this spectacle is flabbergasted.

This precise moment shows the sport-sociological context. According to Weiß, the successful athlete needs the others "to validate the own self, or rather the own identities."

The strong bond that links fans and athletes was particularly apparent at the 2021 US Open final. During the match against Daniil Medvedev, Novak Djokovic burst into tears during the change of sides, and not because he was so devastated by the emerging loss, but because he was so moved by the spectators' support. It hit him completely unexpectedly. After the game, he explained his emotion by saying: "The amount of support, energy and love I got from the crowd was something I will remember forever."

And right away we feel it, too, and understand that titles and records are important to the elite athlete—and Novak Djokovic is certainly a good example of that—but that there is also a second, often hidden level people rarely talk about. Djokovic: "These are the kinds of moments you cherish and these are connections that you establish with people, that will be lasting for a very long time, And yeah, it was just wonderful."

Sports can grant us wonderful moments. Becoming one with the fans, with your teammates, dance partners, sports equipment, the court, the winner's trophy, and with oneself the first time we reach the finish line at a marathon. Many brilliant moments were preceded by a life full of deprivation and lots of training, intuitively following the fifteen minutes of fame proclaimed by Andy Warhol.

Many would not have become what they are if they had not chosen idols. Role models provide guidance and become part of often intuitive goal-setting. "One day I want to play like they do." That is a typical sentence from a child with athletic ambition.

And as a family we followed how Steffi Graf and Boris Becker achieved their success. The tennis boom of the late 1980s and early 1990s grabbed all of us, as we sat fascinated in front of the television. And then I tried to emulate the pros on the court.

My brother, who is five years older than me, was also a role model. Of course, I wanted to do everything just as well as he did. That motivated me and I worked even harder.

But at some point, we have to take the leap and make our own way. "Finding solutions of our own. Figuring out: What are my strengths? Never copying. Being authentic," says Henning Fritz. Ashleigh Barty's mental trainer Ben Crowe's t-shirt read "Embrace your weird" when he watched from the box as his protégé won the Australian Open final in 2022 against US player Danielle Collins.

Embrace your craziness or your differentness, welcome and value your uniqueness—Crowe wears his professional insight on his chest. Like Henning Fritz, he also values first, accepting individuality and second, tailoring any improvement and optimization to the specific personality.

Just like a golf coach must take into account his player's different body and lever relationships, the mental coach looks at the equally deviating mental circumstances and uses the specific individual character as a guiding thread.

"Ash has done a beautiful job." In an interview with *ABC Radio Brisbane*, Crowe explained how he brought out the "human being" in Barty instead of the "human doing."

"The big lesson is to focus on the "human being", and less on the "human doing" and the power of acceptance and gratitude are incredible super powers to enable you to let go of FOOPO[179] and own your story."[180]

Felix Neureuther's understanding of a role model goes even a step further. Back during his active career, he already advocated healthy child development. He continued on this path, and more, after the end of his career. He was even willing to take a direction athletes tend to avoid, of which they are often warned again: to take a political stance.

In the *ARD report* "Spiel mit dem Feuer—Wer braucht dieses Olympia" (Playing with fire—Who needs this Olympia?) aired in January 2022, Neureuther takes a very critical look at the Olympic Games in China. "Something must change for future generations so this precious Olympic idea can survive." During the forty-four-minute report, Neureuther stood in front of the Chinese consulate in Munich and talked to a Uyghur woman. A provocative setting.

Being a role model

Many major sports organizations prefer their players to take a shot on goal rather than a potshot at controversial governments; it would interfere too much in their negotiations with well-off nations as venues for major events. And many athletes oblige them. One of the German national team players who was asked in 1978 in Argentina how he felt about the accusations of torture and potential crimes in nearby prisons, simply replied: "I am not at all interested in the political conditions in Argentina."[181]

It robs the individual of strength while he risks his neck and his job. In 2016, Colin Kaepernick, quarterback for the San Francisco 49ers, chose not to stand for the US national anthem to take a stand against racism. The entire world took notice. The NFL punished him for it and took him off the payroll in 2017.

---

179   Fear Of Other People's Opinions.
180   Suchit (2021).
181   WDR (2015).

By contrast, in 2018, Amnesty International awarded Kaepernick the "Ambassador of Conscience Award" for his action. Many copied Kaepernick's gesture, and not only athletes. The US rapper Eminem took a knee during the globally lionized Superbowl halftime show in 2022. There is no faster way to reach 100 million people.

The soccer player prefers to not acknowledge anything—not depression, not homosexuality, not criticized host locations. Too sensitive, too unpredictable regarding the potential repercussions. Thus, more than a few play an entire career wearing a mask below which they curse, suppress, despair.

It is of absolutely vital importance to quickly make the quantum leap to tolerance and equality to remove this type of totally unnecessary pressure from all affected, and to also allow them the ability to function as an individual and role model once more.

HANDLING MENTAL AND PHYSICAL INJURIES

The images remain in our heads and become uncomfortably engraved in the fans' memories. It hurts to witness, even from a distance, athletes getting injured. How in handball knees and ankles twist, defying the laws of anatomy, how heads slam together in soccer, how high-speed jumps go out of control in downhill ski races. We flinch even in our recliners and bury our face in our hands with a queasy stomach, as though we could unsee it.

When the pop of a torn Achilles tendon echoes through the stadium, it pierces marrow and bone. And anyone who watched in 1981 as the thigh of soccer pro Ewald Lienen was sliced open twenty centimeters by his opponent, still remembers that image today, several decades later.

And the affected athlete not only stores that painful moment but also an image. It can be the traumatic experience from his own perspective, or it can be the original movie one subsequently downloads from the stored television images. But I would warn against the latter as it is not always beneficial to confront oneself early on with frightening images. However, dealing intensively with one's own injury is unavoidable.

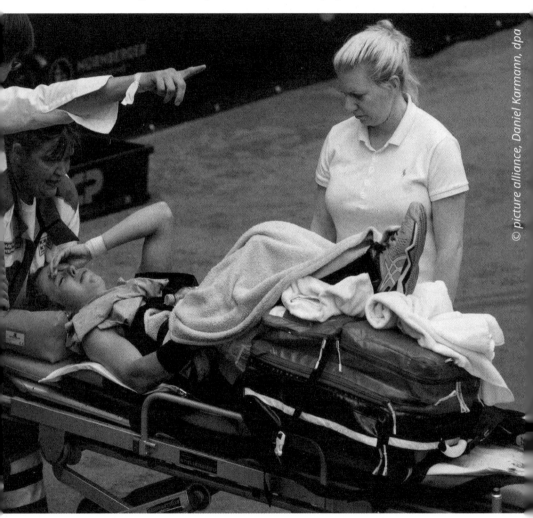

Enduring the most difficult moments and even finding incentive for personal development in them.

© picture alliance, Daniel Karmann, dpa

Injuries are part of professional sports. We train at our limit; the stress and strain of training as well as competing is enormous, especially in tennis where training and tournaments are very closely timed. Tennis is an extreme sport. You can play a tournament every week somewhere in the world. Travel strain, jetlag, lack of sleep, everything is included. Your biorhythm must constantly adjust. We play in different time zones on different surfaces under different climatic conditions. All of that increases the risk of injury.

That makes it all the more important to somehow counter the risk. High-quality, professional training is critical. The athlete and his team need a holistic view of the entire system consisting of body, mind, and environment.

So let us focus on the—with good reason—greatest athletic crisis: the injury. Barely any elite athlete is spared. On the contrary, it is much more likely to get injured during one's career than not.

As far back as the 1990s, the Canadian psychologist Lydia Ievleva together with the Canadian scientist Terry Orlick determined that mental work benefits the healing process. They place special emphasis on the use of **goal-setting**, positive **self-talk**, and **visualization**.[182]

As we saw previously, goal-setting training contributes greatly to maintaining motivation. This is also particularly true within the context of injury because, from the perspective of the affected individual, the many months of regeneration after a severe injury, such as a torn ACL in the knee, is unbearable. This impression is magnified because the chasm

182   Ievleva & Orlick (1991).

between *not being able to move at all and having to move vigorously again at some point* is so great, that one is unable to believe the gap will ever close.

Pitiable are all those who have had to overcome several such injuries already. But at least the torturous moments gifted them some advance knowledge: personally experiencing how to get back on one's legs after such a severe injury, even to work back up to top level, greatly reinforces the belief in one's inner strength and perseverance and can sometimes even inspire.

Disciplined work on regeneration really helps me regain unlimited confidence in the injured body structures. If I give it my all every day to get healthy again, if I work long term with professionals from the various specialized fields—with tennis and fitness trainers, physicians, and physical therapists—I can regain faith in the structures.

I can see small advances, which gives me faith that I can return to my previous level. That helps my mind to remain stable and positive.

The successful process requires ambitious effort. And patience and flexibility. Because the process is rarely linear. Sometimes we swim on top of a wave of euphoria because the scar has healed well, range of motion is steadily improving, and the gait pattern is normalizing. And then an unexpected twinge in the knee pushes us back down into the wave. But most can justifiably look forward to a good rehab program, ultimately flushing them back into the competition venue in a fit state.

We might recognize some helpful parallels if we view the long therapy phase as a long preparation phase for the season, but on crutches. In the first scenario, the end point is the first game, the start of the season. In the other scenario, it is the first competitive start after rehab. The analogy suggests itself.

A small difference that should nevertheless be taken seriously is that the start date of the season is set. But the return date to competition after an injury cannot be set. Setting a deadline as a goal can be very frustrating when it cannot be reached, and it should therefore take a backseat.

Of course, I want to be back on the court after seven months. But first it is more important that, for instance, I am able to bend the knee an additional number of degrees in two weeks.

I can also make my healing process transparent by keeping a weekly chart. The column headers can be important partial aspects, such as kinesthesis and flexion angle. Each weekend I rate these partial aspects on a scale from one to ten. I also add the cross total of all partial aspects in a column on the far right.

I thereby make the progress of each building block visible, but also the overall progress. The latter allows for the values to average out, and a positive progression can still be shown in spite of partial changes for the worse. This moderates potential stagnations and small dents, not to conceal them but to prioritize a holistic view.

Next to result-focused goals—mental goals play a large role. One of the key tasks our injured structure saddles us with: Trust me! But how is that supposed to work?

- The affected ligaments, muscles, bones, and tendons have turned their back on me for months, and now I'm supposed to trust them completely?

- Put all of my bodyweight on them, even let myself fall on them? Lateral movements, pivots, jumps, and spontaneous, unexpected bracing movements?

That is not an undertaking we simply turn on and off. Rather, it is a subtle process that we should initiate carefully and ideally with creative support.

I can imagine movement sequences before I actually initiate them. I prepare them mentally, meticulously run through them, and make an inner movie about how I learn to walk again.

I can prepare every little partial process of my convalescence in this way, all the way to the dynamic handball jump shot against the block of two opposing defenders. My movie reacquaints me with movement patterns and action sequences that have snuck out of my repertoire due to injury.

Properly chosen metaphors can also support my confidence-building measures. Let's imagine a tree at the river whose roots do not go straight down but cling sideways to the embankment. A marvel of strength and effective stability and a role model for every ankle that wants to return to its former strength. When I pair all of this with positive instructions, I have gotten considerably closer to returning to my everyday sport.

For the athlete with injury experience, positive self-talk will possibly happen on its own. They are familiar with the healing process, which, fortunately, often ends well, and believe in it.

There are many studies on how attitude affects the healing of injuries. I always try to bring that to mind during rehabilitation phases, that it isn't just important to train every day, do exercises, and work doggedly on rebuilding the structures that were injured. But also to work on the head, to trust in my work, to look forward with positivity, and to not give up.

Setbacks in rehab are normal. With more serious injuries, it is often two steps forward, one step back. I try to maintain calm and consistent through my daily routines and focus particularly on the positive elements of the rehab process. I want to see the good things, no matter how small.

Unfortunately, the good things are frequently overshadowed by the trauma of past injuries. We get caught up in thoughts we would rather not have. Doubts bubble up, as well as discontentment, and sometimes hopelessness. Images and impressions take hold, and that is unavoidable. While spontaneous thoughts can be erased, images usually remain.

Instead of engaging in a battle that tends to be hopeless, we can also file our life images in a beneficial way. It helps to create a photo album in your head in which you can sort these images. A significant injury event also has its place there. It is up to us when we choose to turn to that page.

Something that sounds so concise provides us with basic internal order. I use the album like a dictionary. I always go to *those* pages that convey the appropriate mood for the respective moment.

It can be the photo of a beaming winner, the focused pose, the cheering spectators. I rarely choose the pages that reflect misfortune and pain. But there are moments for those as well. But not during times of crisis, not before the doctor's diagnosis of yet another injury, and not after a dramatic loss.

But maybe in a phase of strength to remind me of the top performance my body achieved to catapult me back to this level.

The community is an important building block in the process of a swift rehabilitation.

- How does it respond when the athlete has suffered an injury?

- Does everyone support the athlete; does everyone stay in touch?

- The coach, the teammates?

- Does the medical staff offer stability?

It is obvious that the social network has an important rescue function. The family too, and not just the parents but also the siblings.[183]

---

183   Wippert (2002, pg. 196).

A lack of support and a general lack of communication from the social environment quickly leads to uncertainty. It is also important to note that unstable body structures go hand in hand with an unstable psyche.

In addition, there is often the worry that the competition will take advantage of your absence. This is particularly true in team sports where positions are manned by two or three players. If I am the number one starter, I am now understandably worried about this prioritization. And if I am number three, I, of course, worry about whether there is even a place for me once I recover from my injury.

There are simply a lot of highly motivated individuals out there waiting to fill the gap. Emotional and rationally worded support is needed.

Our own environment plays a major role. It is important to have people you trust in your life, people you can talk to when things aren't going so well. People who radiate positivity, who will encourage you, sometimes console you, help you get over worries and fears, and who are simply a positive influence when you are stuck in a deep hole.

Specialists and an optimal infrastructure are extremely important to highly professional rehabilitation. Equally, family and friends, who might not be able to lend professional support, can offer all the more emotional support.

I have relied on a good mix, both during rehab for my ACL tear as well as other injury phases. On the one hand, I made sure to work with experts whom I trust 100 percent and who are absolutely top of their field. On the other hand, it was important to me to use the injury phase to be near my loved ones and my family, and to rehab in a familiar setting.

We cannot get around accepting the injury as part of life in elite sports. But it becomes problematic when acceptance turns into anxiety. Here, anxiety is not only fed by a general concern for one's body, but it also has an existential import. Because an injury can also herald the end of a career. This doesn't automatically suggest occupational disability, but even a permanent performance slump can be enough to bring athletic success to an end.

For me, a certain amount of anxiety and worry about overloading and injuries has always been a part of the sport. I am a very sensitive athlete, and I have paid a lot of attention to my body and thought a lot about why injuries happen to be able to prevent them in the future.

To be able to minimize fear of injuries, I have to know my body really well and trust my judgment. It is important to me to have the freedom to listen to the way I feel at any time, be it during training or at a tournament. I see it this way: My body and I are a team. It sends me signals; it talks to me. It is my job to understand its language, to interpret its clues correctly. Only then am I able to create an optimal stress loading program with my team.

I am not the type to push it. There spossible. Of course, we always want to go higher, faster, and further. But just taking advantage of the body as hard and as long as possible is not my idea of good teamwork, especially not in the long term.

Of course, every pro athlete has phases when they must really grit their teeth, regardless of the sport. That's just part of it. But it has always been extremely important to me that my support team allow me this degree of sensitivity and I am able to make assessing my physical state a part of training and competition control.

WILD CARD

Anyone who thinks injuries are just bad luck is only right to a point. That is, the risk of injury can be lowered through preventive measures. The athlete definitely has to learn to listen closely to his body to notice the rebelling outcry of, for instance, muscle fibers.

- Training volume and intensity may not match the performance level?

- The load increase might have been too erratic?

Careful adjustments are advisable. This list of measures also includes a customized diet, long-term training and competition control, and collaboration between qualified experts: trainers, physical therapists, athletic and mental coaches.

A holistic approach is important for injury prevention. On the physical as well as the mental level. An athlete has to be balanced mentally. In the long term, the athlete must feel neither overwhelmed nor unchallenged and have a lot of motivation and joy in the sport and in achieving the best possible performances. Otherwise, sooner or later, they will suffer physical and mental health problems. When it comes to health, body and mind are closely linked. I had to learn that.

I had several injuries in my career, even as an adolescent. These physical experiences shaped me, and I learned to listen more to my body to be better able to evaluate it and give more thought to what is good for me and what isn't.

I definitely handle injuries differently today than I did ten years ago. As a teenager or young athlete, I considered them more of a curse or an injustice. I thought the body was a machine I could use and expect it to function the way I wanted, all the time.

Today, when my body shows me its limits, I have more sympathy for my own deficiencies and my physical limits. To me, it is not a given that it will always function and bring top performances.

Injury and rehab phases can also make us stronger if we use them correctly. We get some rest and can contemplate some fundamental things, such as motivation:

- *How much does the sport mean to me?*

- *Or about goals: what do I still want to achieve?*

- *Or about our own limits: where are they?*

- *How do I handle them in the future?*

For example, I introduce totally new training stimuli and training content very carefully and with lots of sensitivity. Getting older also causes a stronger physical response to unfamiliar things, which can quickly lead to overstimulation. It is a very personal approach.

Being a professional is a crazy mix of the ability to demand everything from yourself over a long period of time while also being very sensitive and considerate with yourself and your own resources.

Fine-tuning your body and mind to be resilient is a major challenge. The tasks we must master demand a lot of us. The frequency we rarely get to set ourselves—primarily the match and competition calendar—is high. And every new service, every new kickoff creates pressure.

You can read about ways to counter it above. However, sometimes we are not the ones to control the pressure, but it increasingly controls us. Combined with the high frequency of events, we experience the constrictive moments as a repeat loop. Here just a minor injury can feel like a lifesaver.

"Everyone thinks an absence due to injury is horrible. It's not," said Per Mertesacker in a *Spiegel* interview. "Because it is the only way to get a legitimate break, to get off the treadmill."[184]

Loading is followed by unloading, in other words, recovery. When this healthy rhythm is permanently missing, it results in an unhealthy dissonance the body won't accept. If fatigue is so great that rest alone for an imaginary test period of two weeks can no longer overcome it, the diagnosis is usually **overtraining**. And if we break away from strictly sports, we can also call it **burnout**.

The WHO also defines a lack of energy or exhaustion and increasing mental distance from work as negativism and reduced professional efficacy.[185] Many professions have a higher risk of burnout, such as executives and healthcare professionals.[186] The magnitude is enormous and growing.

A projection in Germany for 2019 resulted in approximately 185,000 burnout cases with a total of 4.3 million sick days.[187]

Trainers also have a particularly high burnout risk due to being exposed to so many stressors.[188] The most prominent example in Germany is Ralf Rangnick. He is known for putting a lot of energy into his work. And in 2011, it was finally too much for his mind and his body. The soccer instructor resigned from his positions due to exhaustion.

---

184   Windmann (2018).
185   WHO (2019).
186   Statista Research Department (2022b).
187   Ibidem (2022c).
188   Altfeld & Kellmann (2013).

The pressure that soccer coaches in particular are under is significant. When things aren't going well with the team, *the coach* tends to be the one who has to go. The dismissal is preceded by a heated debate in the media about the coach's strengths and especially weaknesses.

Predictions are quickly made about the number of days the coach has left and which match might become the deciding game. Even before the dismissal is official, the public has been presented with a list of possible successors, even though the public cannot vote on his fate. It's no surprise that soccer trainers have a certain disposition toward burnout.

Next to the trainer, there is, of course, the prominent player who is the focus of media attention, with an open exit door.

- What is circulated about the athlete?

- Does the media create a heroic story with a happy ending?

- Or will the athlete be demoted to a sad hero?

- Or simply torn apart?

Particularly in the tabloids, the hyped-up headline can be followed just weeks later by the unconditional, and by no means always coherent, critique. That's tough to handle.

The pressure is constant and comes from different directions, sometimes direct, sometimes indirect, sometimes more, sometimes less. Here, every sport also follows its own rules and has its own specific list of stressors. Stressors that stir up the orderly process of personal sport-related events: concentration in high-speed sports, perseverance in endurance sports, precision in shooting sports (see fig. 3 for stress factors for golfers).

Stress factors

- Time pressure
- Comments by and conversations with other golfers
- Public sphere
- Misplaced ambition
- Pressure to perform while golfing
  (e.g., drive distances, driving range, putting, playing license, handicap, medal play, tournaments, etc.)
- State of physical fitness
- Old sports injuries
- Lack of mobility
- Physiological problems
  (e.g., high blood pressure, diabetes, overweight, etc.)
- Emotional problems (separation, divorce, death)
- Poor organization
- Hubris
- Sensory overload
- Constant availability
- Fear (of failure or embarrassment)
- Pain
- Conflicts

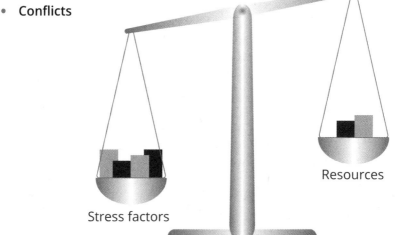

Resources

Stress factors

Fig. 3: Stress factors (Heimsoeth, 2014, pg. 41)

Permanent physical overexertion can also result in burnout. Body and mind correspond on one circuit. Hence, success and failure are not reliable indicators for prognoses.

Let's take the example of the former German national team handball goalkeeper Henning Fritz. Vice-European Champion in 2002, Vice World Champion in 2003, second place at the 2004 Olympics, European Champion in 2004, voted best goalkeeper of the same tournament, and 2004 World Player of the Year. Then, low blow instead of flying high in 2005, burnout.

"I quickly realized that it wasn't just a loss of form; it was something deeper." What made it worse was that, at that time, you weren't able to talk about it openly. Burnout as a socially acceptable symptom of an illness is only gradually being accepted in the industry. We still worry about losing some of our market value when a weakness in our individual mental system is made official.

Fritz found his way back. He searched for a solution for himself. That, too, is an important aspect of our own creative path: being able to navigate it in a solution-focused way and finding a suitable style for the individual. Fritz discovered **frequency-modulated music**, which is based on modulating sounds that don't have to be audible in such a way that they have a positive effect on the vegetative nervous system. It is not scientifically proven but it was helpful to a handball player in need.

Fritz was now third goalkeeper at the THW Kiel, but he was supposed to be number one in the German goal at the 2007 World Championships. The team won the title under trainer Heiner Brand, and after the tournament, Fritz was chosen for the Allstar team. A successful rehabilitation.

It is best to recognize the signs of emerging burnout early and actively work against it. Back in 1984, the psychologist Lazarus introduced a simple as well as plausible four-step formula for stress interpretation and **coping measures**.[189]

---

189   Lazarus & Folkman (1984).

. . . STEP 1:

Interpreting the stressor and categorizing it as "positive," "dangerous," and "irrelevant." Only the dangerous stressor—in the form of a challenge or threat—carries weight. With it, we move on to . . .

. . . STEP 2:

An analysis of my available resources with the options "insufficient" and "adequate." And again, this is only relevant if resources are insufficient. That's when stress happens, and I activate . . .

. . . STEP 3:

Sounding out coping options. If my approach is problem-oriented, I can change the situation myself. By contrast, emotion-focused coping means that I am changing how I relate to the situation and thereby lower the emotions. Next . . .

. . . STEP 4:

I reflect on how I got a handle on the at-first dangerous stressor. If my conclusion is positive, I might just see a challenge. If my coping strategy failed, I am dealing with a threat for which I must find new measures, possibly also simply avoiding the situation.

Lazarus's **transactional stress model** clearly shows that the stress experience is largely influenced by us. Our own judgment determines whether the stress will turn into a negative threat or a positive challenge. What matters is which resources we have at our disposal, meaning how resilient we are and what tools we have for taking countermeasures.

Such tools would be, for instance, the ability to change perspectives or to regulate our emotions via relaxation techniques. Hans Eberspächer focuses the authors' reaction patterns on flight, bearing up, and challenge.[190]

---

190   Eberspächer (2011).

But none of these things would be suitable as a permanent solution, especially continuously bearing up, which has the potential to lead to burnout. But living in permanent challenge mode is also not the solution. Eberspächer considers top performers to be all those who are able to "flexibly use the entire spectrum of possible coping strategies and their variations."

Being mindful of our basic needs

Here, flight should not be seen as a negative emergency solution, but should be considered a strategic measure. The psychologist makes an appeal to all of us to pay attention to our basic needs, listing nutrition, exercise, regeneration, relaxation, and sleep as the basic physical needs, while self-management, self-worth, self-determination, attachment, pleasure, joy, diversion and entertainment are listed as basic mental needs.

And just as the physically injured individual is surrounded by a team of carers to ensure their professional physical rehabilitation, the mentally overexerted individual needs a social environment that provides support and continuity. And that can just be simply listening in close proximity and giving the affected individual the opportunity to share his thoughts.

When I could only do mindless exercise-band rehab exercises for weeks because my knee was not yet capable of more, I stumbled from one motivational hole to the next. I asked myself every day:

How long and especially how many more times do I have to go through these phases? Sometimes I practically dragged myself to the fitness studio, dreading the same old exercises before I even got there. They were so far removed from what I actually wanted to do. Everything seemed miserable.

> *But one good trait helps me here: I never quit. Never! When it gets to the point where I am so incredibly unmotivated, I take the time for an inner motivational talk. I appeal to my patience and tenacity and tell myself where I am right now and where I want to go.*
>
> *I explain to myself that not wanting to do monotonous exercise-band exercises is also an important sign because it tells me how much fire I have in my belly for my real task. And, being able to overcome such tough phases is a sign of strength.*
>
> *I imagine that this stagnation phase is meant to test my willpower. Do I really want to fight my way back? And when I determine honestly how much I want to get back to being fit to play at the highest level, I have passed the test.*
>
> *And then I realize how important it is to work on the little things that add up over time and turn into something big. Even if right now it doesn't look like it at all.*

SAFEGUARDING THE QUALITY OF A CAREER

The harsh realization: The amount of money an athlete earns is not determined primarily by talent, support, and training discipline. It is determined primarily by the type of sport. Those fortunate enough to excel in soccer, tennis, or golf, and in the United States, possibly basketball, football, and ice hockey, hit the jackpot. *Especially*, and sometimes *only*, if they are male. In many sports, women are still paid less, and sometimes not at all.

The exchange rate is determined by the television ratings and click rate, meaning the consumer in front of a screen. And the spectator tends to favor those athletes who run the fastest, jump the highest, throw the furthest, and shoot the hardest. The ratios shift in tennis, in swimming, in some winter sports, and in disciplines with greater aesthetics. Women experience more media and financial equality here. Apart from that, inequality persists.

Thus, earnings often don't even depend on the success level. Guesstimate: What does a four-time European champion, four-time World Champion, and two-time Olympic silver-medalist earn? The cash should, of course, flow.

But that flow abruptly stops if the athlete is a bobsledder. He makes less than a minor-league soccer player who has never been invited to play on a national team, much less participated at the Olympics. Johannes Lochner, one of the world's best bobsledders, has to work in his family's electrician business so he can continue to speed down the ice canal without financial hardship.[191]

Financial independence makes performance easier

So, money plays a major role in planning a career, and the amount of time someone can earn money as an active athlete is limited. In many sports, the career ends in the mid-thirties. And had I been an artistic cyclist, hardly anyone would have known.

Another guesstimate: Who knows the name of the current World Champion in artistic cycling? And since hardly anyone is interested in this highly aesthetic, artistic, and athletic form of cycling, it is not televised. And no sponsor will support something no one watches. So, the money supply remains cut off even though German media should be interested in the fact that at the last thirty-five World Championships (as of 2021), the title went to the German men thirty-four times and German women twenty-seven times.

But even when the money flows, competing in elite sports remains a precarious endeavor, at least for the individual athlete because there are lots incalculable factors. Expenditure is high for participating at the top level and must be paid in advance.

---

191   ARD (2022).

Tennis for example: a professional team is necessary and large, consisting of a trainer, fitness coach, physical therapist, nutritionist, and psychologist.

While top ten players can afford to be permanently surrounded by such a gaggle of experts and bring them to tournaments as their entourage, the pretty-good-but-just-not-as-good players must make a tough calculation.

And if we disregard the sponsor benefits, there is no regular income. Because earnings from tournament prize money is not a reliable asset, no one knows how far the athlete will get. It's like working 100 percent on commission. Not desirable.

Next to money from sponsors, Johannes Lochner at least has the money he earns in his family business as a reserve. The organization Deutsche Sporthilfe (German Athletes' Support) is another income source, but of merely a couple hundred Euros per month. But that usually doesn't even cover the rent. In Germany, for example, only those who are able to get a civil service job, such as customs or federal border police, and are largely released from duty for the sport, receive solid core funding.

This results in stress suffered by a shocking number of athletes, as a study of more than 1,000 Olympic and Paralympic athletes shows: A third of athletes have too little money to be able to properly focus on their sport.[192]

Since money is a major factor in athletic development, athletes must constantly make unpleasant compromises and, for instance, participate in the Olympics for a country they really would rather not support. But only there can they find concentrated media attention and suddenly appear on a global screen, which can bring lucrative sponsor contracts.

---

192   Deutsche Sporthilfe (2021).

So there goes that **autonomy** we unanimously agreed on earlier. We must reclaim it, strengthen the individual, and create a foundation for the so important autonomous athlete.

Fritz Henning, the 2004 World Handball Player of the Year, emphasizes this as well. "Everyone has to find their own style," is his recommendation for all who wish to go far in a sport.

Some things just have to mature and evolve over the years. As a young girl, I trained really hard because it is what I wanted to do. When my coach told me at age twelve to run forty minutes of hills and stairs at the Metzingen vineyards, I did it for an hour. My heart rate was supposed to peak at 190, but my inner goal was to break 200.

Back then, my father stood at the foot of the stairs and timed me or tallied my runs. Today he says he felt so sorry for me as he watched me pant and struggle. But there was no reason for that. I was in my element and convinced that it was the only way to make it big.

As an adolescent, up until I was a young adult, I toiled and asked more of my body than it could offer. I was convinced that someday I would reap the reward. But that's not what happened. I had lots of injuries early on, resulting in frequent limitations during daily training, setbacks, and too little consistency in training and tournaments.

I got frustrated, doubted my performance capacity and my physical qualifications. And at some point, fortunately, my plan, which didn't really work.

Only later in my career, when I was in my mid-twenties, did I learn to pay more attention to my body and my needs. I began to consider my mental state during physical training. For example, I learned to not to train so hard when I didn't feel 100 percent fit or was very stressed.

Since my body was very sensitive to training stimuli, I started by considerably reducing my training volume but training at significantly higher intensities. Better only two hours of tennis a day but with full concentration and maximum intensity. The same in fitness training: high intensity training in all areas.

And the very hard but shorter training suddenly resulted in more time for rest and regeneration, and even more free time.

I realized how much I had gotten myself wedged in training hard over the years and how little I had valued my well-being. I noticed that on some days, it is better for me to skip a tough unit and instead take a relaxed run through the woods and enjoy nature.

On other days, when I would theoretically just have a relaxed unit on the schedule, I might have felt that I had a lot more left and turned it into a hard interval unit. Not because someone told me to, but because I wanted it and noticed that, at that moment, mind and body were willing.

Committing oneself uncompromisingly to performance sports and training discipline can certainly lead to success, but it can also negatively affect development. According to scientist Anke Abraham, the "more exclusively we fixate on performance sports and the fewer life alternatives we develop, the greater is the risk of identity loss and mental collapse when the athlete is no longer available to 'deliver' identity certainty."[193]

---

193   Abraham (2008, pg. 243).

I always thought it important not to forget that there are other things in life outside of tennis. Hence, I also viewed the circuit as a journey and used it to gain a better understanding of the world and expand my horizons. In 2016, I was just able to qualify for the Olympics in Rio—a dream was coming true.

But even in Rio, I didn't want to just see tennis courts. So, I arrived a week earlier to spend that time with friends, a German-Brazilian family. I immersed myself in the life of the locals and became acquainted with an extraverted city. And I was also perfectly acclimated when the Olympic tournament started.

Later, many departed immediately after they were eliminated to return to the circuit as quickly as possible and prepare for the US Open. I passed on possible prize money to spend an additional week in the Olympic village. I was able to meet other athletes and build new friendships, some of which continue today. We watched competitions together.

Watching the best German athletes from many different sports up close from the front row and cheer them on was an opportunity I might never have again. It was very special, something I will remember for the rest of my life.

In the end, those three weeks in Rio were some of the best I have experienced in my sport. Many said I was crazy when I canceled subsequent tournaments in Cincinnati and New Haven. But I arrived at the US Open in a great mood and, of course, on time. And I won the mixed title with Mate Pavić. Probably also because my mental state was excellent.

Not allowing others to take control, to put up with being called crazy, and also accepting a considerable financial loss is all to the credit of a mature top athlete.

- Which social media post will I agree to?

- Which advertising vehicle will I allow myself to be hitched to for a testimonial?

- Which insurance company, which bookies, which airline fits my personality and my life principles?

Money for prestige in a world without discipline—all too often we see actions based on this model. Commercialization has steamrolled and flattened the original athletic ethos: sportsmanship. Many things are the same and have thus become exchangeable. Even the course of a career must fit in a standard mold.

There was much astonishment when Philip Lahm announced the end of his career one year earlier than expected, but the reasons were obvious. The exceptional defender, whom coach Pep Guardiola once called the most intelligent player he ever coached, wrote on his Facebook page on February 8, 2017: "As captain it is important to me to bring a top performance at every training session and every game. I know that I am not able to do so for another season beyond the current one."[194]

Another example: The biathlete Laura Dahlmeier. Her Wikipedia entry says "retired." Yet she was only born in 1993. She announced her retirement at age twenty-five. A bomb shell announcement, because the two-time Olympic gold medalist and seven-time World Champion surely could have collected much more hardware.

This kind of determination might be in the female biathletes' DNA, because Magdalena Neuner was twenty-five when she ended her legendary biathlon career. She had already won the overall World Cup at age twenty-one and was a two-time Olympic champion as well as a twelve-time World Champion.

---

194   Lahm (2022).

"I simply realized I had reached a line I did not want to cross. I had trained for so long. Investing that much again, spending another nine months away from home, pulling off all of that with consistency?! The thought alone felt exhausting."

Maintaining control over one's life is what is needed. And that's clearly the plan for this twenty-five-year-old top athlete. The most recent example is Ashleigh Barty, who announced her retirement on February 23, 2022 on Instagram, at the age of twenty-five, with the words: "I'm so happy and I'm so ready." She, too, was at the top in the world, ranked number one. She had won the French Open, and then, her dream, winning on the "sacred" Wimbledon green grass. All that was missing was the Australian Open on native soil.

When she had managed that, too, she had reached the end of an amazing journey. In her words: "I know that the time is right now for me to step away and chase other dreams." And there was another statement that was rarely quoted—that she had learned not to put the results ahead of everything else: "My happiness wasn't dependent on the results." What mattered to her was feeling like she had given it everything she had. And now the next phase of her life begins, not as an athlete but as a human being.

Planned retirements, such as those already discussed, are generally processed pretty quickly, unlike *unplanned* ends to a career. According to scientist Pia-Maria Wippert, "with a lack of support and a high degree of stress, they [athletes] are potentially unable to cope for years and in some instances for the rest of their life," and they can end up suffering from PTSD and exhaustion-related crises.[195]

A study with 194 former professional soccer players, whose careers ended on average four years prior, evidenced psychopathological symptoms. A total of 29 percent of test subjects exhibited symptoms of anxiety and depression and another 28 percent suffered from insomnia.[196]

---

195   Wippert (2008, pg. 254).
196   Ramele et al. (2017).

It was the phase between ages 18 and 23: The more I played in the smaller ITF tournaments and the more the results I wanted so desperately to achieve failed to materialize, the more disillusioned but also ambitious and grimly determined I became. Professional tennis leaves many victims in its wake. Traveling forty weeks a year, always away from friends and family, constant training and tournaments virtually without a break from January until the end of October, then two weeks of vacation, and right back to the tough preparation for the new year. There is barely any rest.

In addition, we have to defend points every week to confirm our playing level, or we quickly slide down the ranking list. All of that comes with a high degree of mental strain.

My career stagnated, I was ranked between 200 and 350 on the world ranking list. I had always imagined more for myself and thought I was capable of more. I was incredibly frustrated by not making better and faster progress.

Then came a good phase: I cracked the top-200 mark. I thought I would feel better after reaching this milestone and everything would improve. But the opposite happened. During that time, my emotional state was worse than ever. Even as a top-200 player, with that prize money I still couldn't afford to hire a trainer who could have accompanied me full-time to the tournaments and helped me improve my game.

It was torture always traveling to tournaments by myself. The worst part was always feeling like the conditions were never ideal for showcasing my potential.

During that time, when my ranking was the best it had ever been, I realized that the ladder to success that I had always imagined had no end. That every peak we finally crest turns out to be merely a transition to the next, higher mountain.

I was no longer able to enjoy my journey and in my mid-twenties decided to dedicate my life to things that brought me more joy and satisfaction. Against nearly all advice, I exited the rat race and thus my life as a tennis pro.

© picture alliance, Marijan Murat, dpa

The extreme sport of tennis: between the limelight and an existence as a solo combatant.

WILD CARD

The end of a career, even if planned, should be prepared. The scientist Dorothee Alfermann[197] together with her colleagues asked 254 athletes from Germany, Lithuania, and Russia to rate the end of their career in hindsight.

The predominant coping strategy was acceptance. And it turned out that an anticipated preparation would be beneficial. This should include defining the reasons for retirement, setting a convenient time, then making plans for the future, and checking to see which resources the athlete can use to manage the transition phase. But more than a few do return after announcing their retirement.

When I retired, I did not think it possible that I would ever return to professional tennis as an active player. The two years when, for the first time in my life, tennis wasn't my top priority, were liberating.

I enjoyed feeling settled at home in Stuttgart, the ordinary life in the now without having to prove each week that you're one of the best or want to be one of them at all costs. I focused on my psychology studies and got my coaching license for the German Tennis Federation. My studies, my coaching training, and working as a coach at the club level gave me an entirely new perspective of the sport.

Even today, I am not exactly sure how my return to the circuit came about. I had never stopped training for myself, both on the court and at the fitness studio. I simply love playing a sport.

But for the very first time, I allowed myself to experiment, to not stick to any plans, not have a specific goal, but to simply do what was good for me and excited me. I changed my diet and tried out new training methods I had learned about in my coaching training.

---

197   Alfermann et al. (2004).

During this process, I was my own guinea pig and learned to better listen to my body and my mind. I was no longer interested in perfection. I wanted to optimize my game, which was important to me.

And I never stopped playing small ITF tournaments because I did not want to lose my place on the ranking list entirely. It is relevant to how much we earn in various national leagues in Europe, and tennis was always supposed to remain a source of income for me.

So, I played regional tournaments, and once I had stopped taking the matches seriously, I suddenly began to win. It was strange.

Sometimes I felt almost cheated. All my life, I had done everything for tennis, and now, when it no longer mattered, I was getting the results I had always wanted. And thus, I moved, bit by bit, up the ranking list.

In 2015, I completed my Bachelor's degree in general psychology and decided to give my professional career another chance.

As the legendary basketball player Kobe Bryant said: "The key is to be aware of how you feel and how you should feel. Everything starts with awareness."[198]

Ashleigh Barty also allowed herself a time out, played cricket, and came back strong. Individuality creates growth, and that leads to success. Only after her self-prescribed break from tennis did Barty win the Grand Slam titles in Paris, Wimbledon, and Melbourne. And only after her withdrawal did Laura Siegemund win the US Open in doubles and mixed doubles.

Kobe Bryant, who thought so much about body and mind, and about the opponent and himself, summarized it so perfectly:
"You can't achieve greatness by walking a straight line."

---

198   Bryant (2019, pg. 31–33).

SUMMARY

Careers have many time windows: competition day, the season, or the years-long active phase before retirement. This final point can be determined by various factors, such as injuries and age, but also by an inner desire. Where does such a desire come from? What drives the athlete?

PROMISING

Wanting to continue to grow *** setting your own standards *** creating inner success as a prerequisite for outer success *** making a checklist of the things that matter to you *** learning more from mistakes than from successes *** not forcing success *** visualizing success.

SEARCHING FOR MEANING AND FINDING YOUR IDENTITY

Recognition as incentive *** having role models and being a role model *** developing your own style *** being authentic *** overcoming the pressure of conformism.

PROCESSING PHYSICAL AND MENTAL INJURIES

Turning to preventive measures *** incorporating self-talk and visualization *** goal-setting training *** creating a mood rating scale *** matching stress factors to resources *** organizing your social and professional environment *** differentiating stressors as a measure against burnout.

SAFEGUARDING THE QUALITY OF A CAREER

Maintaining autonomy *** seeing not just the performance sport, but also the person *** accepting interruptions *** normalizing unconventional trajectories.

© picture alliance, Marijan Murat, dpa

© picture alliance, Diorgenes Pandini, dpa

MATCH ANALYSIS

ON THE WAY TO THE LOCKER ROOM— THE AUTHORS' CLOSING CONVERSATION

Our book is now coming to an end—our own, exciting match. What is your final analysis, Laura?

Very positive, Stefan! It was like a tennis tournament, just as real and suspenseful. We were confronted with demanding situations, had to classify them, respond to them, and resolve them. Always with an opportunity for growth and reward.

So "real." I like that description. Only four letters, but a very promising motto that urges authenticity, finding one's own style and path, being honest with oneself.

Exactly. We pay more attention to the individual without losing sight of the general regularities. We encounter these two levels all the time. I like comparing it with biomechanics in tennis. There are many different, personal stroke techniques. They range from distinct to peculiar. And yet every stroke has certain intersections that are identical with all top players. Such are the laws of physics.

The goal is to connect these two levels prudently to create a personal success strategy.

I think we can close with these words.

It was my pleasure to play balls back and forth with you. What is it we say at the net when we shake hands?

When it was a great game like ours? Thanks, great match!

REFERENCES

Abraham, A. (2008). Identitätsbildungen im und durch Sport. In K. Weis & P. Gugutzer, *Handbuch Sportsoziologie* (S. 239-248). Hofmann: Schorndorf.

Agassi, A. (2009). *Open – das Selbstporträt.* Droemer: München.

Alfermann, D., Stambulova, N., & Zemaityte, A. (2004). Reactions to sport career termination: A cross-national comparison of German, Lithuanian, and Russian athletes. *Psychology of Sport and Exercise, 5(1)*, 61-75.

Altfeld, S., & Kellmann, M. (2013). Burnout bei Trainern. *Zeitschrift für Sportpsychologie 20(2)*, 47-58.

Amez, S., Baert, S., Neyt, B. & Vandemaele, M. (2020). No evidence for second leg home advantage in recent seasons of European soccer cups. *Applied Economics Letters. 27(2)*, 156-160. https://biblio.ugent.be/publication/8619662, Einsicht am: 1.7.2021.

Antonovsky, A. (1997). *Salutognese: Zur Entmystifizierung der Gesundheit.* DGVT-Verlag: Tübingen.

ARD (2022) – Reportage *„Spiel mit dem Feuer – Wer braucht dieses Olympia?".*

Barschel, Ch. A. (2015). https://www.tennisnet.com/news/australian-open-als-sich-tommy-haas-selbst-beschimpfte-33267 (1.2.2015), Einsicht am: 27.3.2022.

Baumeister, R. F. (1984). Choking under pressure: Self-consciousness and paradoxical effects of incentives on skillful performance. *Journal of Personality and Social Psychology, 46(3)*, 610-620.

Beckmann, J. (2015). *Mentales Training im Golf.* Spitta: Balingen.

Beckmann, J., & Elbe, A.-M. (2008). *Praxis der Sportpsychologie im Wettkampf- und Leistungssport.* Spitta: Balingen.

Beckmann-Waldenmayer, D., & Beckmann, J. (2012). *Handbuch sportpsychologischer Praxis.* Spitta: Balingen.

Bogner (o. J.). https://www.bogner.com/de-de/bogner-world/ambassadors/bernhard-langer.html, Einsicht am: 14.4.2021.

Brand, H., & Löhr, J. (2008). *Projekt Gold.* Gabal: Offenbach.

Brecht, B. (o. J.). http://zitate.net, Einsicht am: 23.2.2022.

Bruhn, H., Kopiez, R., & Lehmann, A. C. (2008). *Musikpsychologie.* Rowohlt: Reinbek.

Brunner, S. (2020). Ein Mensch, der immer 100 Prozent gibt. *green, 1*, 50.

Brunner, S. (2019). „Niemals aufgeben!" *green, 1*, 54.

Brunner, S. (2017a). Der knifflige Umgang mit Druck. *Süddeutsche Zeitung*, 29.5.2017.

Brunner, S. (2017b). Jazz – ein Genre ohne Alternative. *green, 2*, 83.

Brunner, S. (2002). *Verarbeitung von Schulstress bei Jugendlichen.* Logos Verlag: Berlin.

Brunner, S. (1998). Alte Socken und karierte Unterhosen. *Süddeutsche Zeitung, 20./21.6.1998*, II.

Brunner, S. (1988): *Subjektive Theorien Erwachsener über ihre Nichtteilnahme an sportlicher Aktivität* (Diplomarbeit).

Brunstein, C. (1993). Personal goals and subjective well-being: A longitudinal study. *Journals of Personality and Social Psychology, 65*, 1061-1070.

Bryant, K. (2019). *Mamaba Mentality.* Riva: München.

Bundesinstitut für Arzneimittel und Medizinprodukte (2019). ICD-10-WHO. https://www.dimdi.de/static/de/klassifikationen/icd/icd-10-who/kode-suche/htmlamtl2019/block-f10-f19.htm, Einsicht am: 31.3.2022.

Burchard, S. (2015). *Spiel dein bestes Tennis.* Aachen: Meyer & Meyer Verlag.

Catuogno, C. (2019). „Hallo Wasser. Ich bin die Britta". *Süddeutsche Zeitung*, 22.7.2019.

Csikszentmihalyi, M. (2017). *Flow – das Geheimnis des Glücks.* Klett-Cotta: Stuttgart.

Csikszentmihalyi, M. (1975). *Beyond boredom and anxiety.* Jossey-Bass: San Francisco.

Czycholl, H. (2020). *Gibt es einen Heimvorteil? Warum?* DFB, https://www.dfb.de/vereinsmitarbeiter/abteilungsleiterin-fussball/artikel/gibt-es-einen-heimvorteil-warum-1457/, Einsicht am: 1.3.2022.

Damasio, A. R. (1994). *Descartes' Irrtum – Fühlen, Denken und das menschliche Gehirn.* München: List.

Deutsche Sporthilfe (2021). *Deutschlands Spitzensportler:innen benötigen bessere Rahmenbedingungen.* https://www.sporthilfe.de/ueber-uns/medien/pressemitteilungen/studie-deutschlands-spitzenportlerinnen-benoetigen-bessere-rahmenbedingungen (6.11.2021), Einsicht am: 17.11.2021.

Digitalphoto (2018). https://www.digitalphoto.de/news/macht-bilder-was-fotos-uns-bewegen-100341501.html (21.3.2018), Einsicht am: 5.3.2022.

Dunne, S., Chib, V. S., Berleant, J., & O'Doherty, J. P. (2018). Reappraisal of incentives ameliorates choking under pressure and is correlated with changes in the neural representations of incentives. *Social Cognitive and Affective Neuroscience, 14(1)*, 13-22.

Eberspächer, H. (2012). *Mentales Training.* Stiebner Verlag: München.

Eberspächer, H. (2011). *Gut sein, wenn's drauf ankommt.* Carl Hanser: München.

Ehlert, R. G. (o. J.). https://musikwissenschaften.de/lexikon/m/motiv/, Einsicht am: 2.2.2022.

Engbert, K. (2017). *Mentales Training im Leistungssport.* Neuer Sportverlag: Stuttgart.

Eurosport (2022). https://www.eurosport.de/tennis/australian-open/2022/daniil-medvedev-viertelfinale-felix-auger-aliassime-grand-slam-melbourne-halbfinale-stefanos-tsitsip_sto8739391/story.shtml, Einsicht am: 27.1.2022.

Frank, R. (2008). *Glück.* Patmos: Düsseldorf.

Gallwey, W. T. (2015). *The inner game of golf.* Pan Macmillan: Basingstoke, England.

Gallwey, W. T. (2012): *Tennis – Das innere Spiel.* Wilhelm Goldmann Verlag: München.

Gatzmaga, N., Thrien, H., Thrien, F., & Borgmann, S. (2020). *Mentales Training mit Vorbildern im Sport.* Spitta: Balingen.

Gesamtverband der Deutschen Versicherungswirtschaft (2018). *„Man hat nur eine Chance, eine Sprengung durchzuführen".* https://www.gdv.de/de/themen/positionen-magazin/-man-hat-nur-eine-chance-eine-sprengung-durchzufuehren--39622 (1.3.2018), Einsicht am: 13.2.2022.

Gladwell, M. (2009). *Outliers – the story of success.* Hachette Book Group: New York.

Goleman, D. (1980). 1528 geniuses and how they grew. *Psychology Today*, 28-53.

Gotzner, P. (2016). https://www.helmholtz.de/newsroom/artikel/der-hoechste-druck/, Einsicht am: 8.6.2020.

Graf, S. (2022). https://twitter.com/SteffiGraf40/status/429551538546425856, Einsicht am: 25.2.2022.

Greenwald, J. (2007). *The best tennis of your life.* Penguin Random House: New York.

Gröninger, S., & Stade-Gröninger, J. (1996). *Progressive Relaxation.* J. Pfeiffer Verlag: München.

Güllich, A., & Krüger, M. (2013). *Sport.* Springer: Berlin.

Hanin, Y. L. (2000). Individual zones of optimal functioning (IZOF) model. Emotion-performance relationships in sport. In Y. L. Hanin (Ed.), *Emotions in sport* (pp. 65-89). Human Kinetics: Champaign, IL, USA.

Hauschild, J. (2020). *Sagen Sie mal, Frau Boshammer: Sollten wir alles verzeihen?* https://www.psychologie-heute.de/leben/artikeldetailansicht/40809-sagen-sie-mal-frau-boshammer-sollten-wir-alles-verzeihen.html (9.10.2020), Einsicht am: 28.2.2022.

Heckhausen, H., Gollwitzer, P., & Weinert, F. (1987): *Jenseits des Rubikon: Der Wille in den Humanwissenschaften.* Springer-Verlag: Berlin.

Heimsoeth, A. (2014). *Golf mental.* Pietsch: Stuttgart.

Herrigel, E. (2011). *ZEN in der Kunst des Bogenschießens.* O. W. Barth: München.

Hopper, D. (2021). „Wenn es gut läuft, ist man hier der König." *Süddeutsche Zeitung*, 21.12.2021.

Ievleva, L., & Orlick, T. (1991). Mental links to enhanced healing: An exploratory study. *The Sport Psychologist, 5(1)*, 25-40.

Jablinski, D. (2021). Ein längeres Leben durch Smartphone Anwendungen und Aktivitätstracker? *Zeitschrift für Sportpsychologie, Jg. 28*, Heft 3, 122.

Jacobson, E. (2011). *Entspannung als Therapie.* Klett-Cotta: Stuttgart.

Jansen, P., & Hoja, S. (2018). Macht Sport wirklich glücklich? *Zeitschrift für Sportpsychologie, 25(1)*, 21-32.

Kästner, E. (o. J.). *Lob des Tennisspiels.* http://www.sportunterricht.de/lksport/kaestner.html, Einsicht am: 13.1.22.

King, B. J. (2008). *Pressure is a privilege: Lessons I've learned from life and the battle of the sexes.* Life time Media: New York.

Kingston, K., & Hardy, L. (1997). Effects of different types of goals on processes that support performance. *The Sport Psychologist, 11*, 289.

Kittler, Ch. (2019). Unter Druck entstehen Diamanten. *Zeitschrift für Sportpsychologie, 26 (3)*, 142.

Kleinert, J., & Sulprizio, M. (2019). Motivation und Zielsetzung. In K. Staufenbiehl et al., *Angewandte Sportpsychologie für den Leistungssport* (S. 173-187). Hogrefe: Göttingen.

Kreienbühl, Ch. (2018). *Wie sich ein Marathon anfühlt.* https://ckr.ch/2018/12/08/ckrblog-wie-sich-ein-marathon-anfuehlt/ (8.12.2018), Einsicht am: 25.1.2022.

Lahm, Ph. (2022). https://www.facebook.com/PhilippLahm/photos/a.251642919388/10154414229829389/?type=3&_rdr, Einsicht am: 28.3.2022.

Lazarus, R. S., & Folkman, S. (1984). *Stress, appraisal, and coping.* Springer Publishing: New York.

Linz, L. (2014). *Erfolgreiches Teamcoaching.* Meyer und Meyer: Aachen.

Matschnig, M. (2007). *Körpersprache.* Gräfe und Unzer: München.

McAngus Todd, N. P. (2000). Vestibular responses to loud dance music: A physiological basis of the "rock and roll threshold". *The Journal of the Acoustical Society of America, 107*, 496.

Mehrabian, A. (1971): *Silent messages* (p.43). Wadsworth Publishing Company: Belmont, California, USA.

Memmert, D., & Leiner, S. (2020). *Tennisspiele werden im Kopf entschieden.* Meyer & Meyer Verlag: Aachen.

Messner, R. (o. J.). www.beruhmte-zitate.de, Einsicht am: 25.3.2022.

Michaelsen, S. (2022). „Die Schauspielerei ist ein Angstberuf". *Magazin der Süddeutschen Zeitung*, 14.1.2022.

Molcho, S. (1988). *Körpersprache als Dialog.* Mosaik Verlag: München.

Morgenthaler, Ch., & Hauri, R. (2010). *Rituale im Familienleben. Inhalte, Formen und Funktionen im Verhältnis der Generationen.* Juventa Verlag: Weinheim (Abstract).

Müsseler, J., & Rieger, M. (2017). *Allgemeine Psychologie.* Springer-Verlag: Berlin.

Mumm, J. et al. (2020). *Auftrittsängste bei Musikerinnen und Musikern.* Göttingen: Hogrefe.

Myers, D. G. (2008). *Psychologie.* Heidelberg: Springer Medizin Verlag.

Neave, N., & Wolfson, S. (2003): Testosterone, territoriality, and the "home advantage" *Physiology & Behavior 78*(2), 269-275.

Neue Szene (2018). *Die größten Underdog-Siege nach Quoten.* https://www.neue-szene.de/magazin/sport/die-größten-underdog-siege-nach-quoten (28.5.2018), Einsicht am: 18.1.22.

Nideffer, R. M. (1967). *The Inner Athlete* (pp. 52-57). Ty Crowell Co: New York.

Paasch, R. (2015). *Selbstwirksamkeit im Fußball.* https://www.die-sport-psychologen.de/2015/08/dr-rene-paasch-selbstwirksamkeit-im-fuss-ball/ (25.8.2015), Einsicht am: 13.3.2022.

Puni, A. Z. (1961). *Abriss der Sportpsychologie.* Berlin: Sportverlag.

Raab, M., Gula, B., & Gigerenzer, G. (2012). The hot hand exists in Volleyball and is used for allocation decisions. *Journal of Experimental Psychology-Applied, 18*(1), 81-94.

Ramele, S. van, Aoki. H., Kerkhoffs, G. M., & Gouttebarge, V. (2017). Mental health in retired professional football players: 12-month incidence, adverse life events and support. *Psychology of Sport an Exercise, 28*, 85-90.

Ran (2021). *Barty nach Wimbledon-Sieg demütig: „Wichtiger, ein guter Mensch zu sein".* https://www.ran.de/tennis/grand-slam/wimbledon/news/barty-nach-wimbledonsieg-demuetig-wichtiger-ein-guter-mensch-zu-sein-126302 (11.7.2021), Einsicht am: 24.3.2022.

Regel, N. (2021). „Es geht darum, selbstbestimmt zu leben". *Süddeutsche Zeitung*, 3.12.2021.

Rendschmidt, M., & Friebe, M. (2020). *„Manche haben nur einmal die Chance auf Olympia".* Deutschlandfunk, https://www.deutschlandfunk.de/corona-und-olympia-manche-haben-nur-einmal-die-chance-auf-100.html (21.3.2020), Einsicht am: 4.2.2022.

Röthig, P., & Prohl, R. (2003). *Sportwissenschaftliches Lexikon.* Hofmann-Verlag: Schorndorf.

Shaw, B. (o. J.). http://zitate.net/erfolg-zitate, Einsicht am: 25.3.2022.

Stangl, W. (2022). *Rumination. In Online-Lexikon für Psychologie und Pädagogik,* https://lexikon.stangl.eu/4167/rumination, Einsicht am: 5.3.2022.

Statista Research Department (2012). https://de.statista.com/statistik/daten/studie/233475/umfrage/praevalenz-von-burn-out-nach-geschlecht-alter-und-sozialem-status/, Einsicht am: 3.12.2021.

Statista Research Department (2020). https://de.statista.com/infografik/1171/erwerbstaetige-in-deutschland-mit-nebenjob/, Einsicht am: 19.1.2022.

Statista Research Department (2022a). https://de.statista.com/statistik/daten/studie/793787/umfrage/umfrage-zu-den-guten-vorsaetzen-fuer-das-neue-jahr-in-deutschland/, Einsicht am: 5.2.2022.

Statista Research Department (2022b). https://de.statista.com/statistik/daten/studie/239672/umfrage/berufsgruppen-mit-den-meisten-fehltagen-durch-burn-out-erkrankungen/ Einsicht am: 5.2.2022.

Statista Research Department (2022c). https://de.statista.com/statistik/daten/studie/239872/umfrage/arbeitsunfaehigkeitsfaelle-aufgrund-von-burn-out-erkrankungen/ Einsicht am: 5.2.2022.

Statista Research Department (2022d). https://de.statista.com/statistik/daten/studie/384680/umfrage/verteilung-des-reichtums-auf-der-welt/ Einsicht am: 3.2.2022.

Staufenbiel, K., Liesenfeld, M., & Lobinger, B. (2019). *Angewandte Sportpsychologie für den Leistungssport.* Hogrefe: Göttingen.

Suchit, H. (2021). *Essentially sports.* https://www.essentiallysports.com/wta-tennis-news-focus-on-the-human-being-mindset-coach-reveals-how-ashleigh-barty-deals-with-external-pressure/ (19.7.2021), Einsicht am: 29.2.2022.

Tagesschau (2021). *Keine „spontane Weltrettung" in Sicht.* https://www.tagesschau.de/inland/schulze-klimakonferenz-103.html (13.102021), Einsicht am: 13.3.2022.

Vieweg, W. (2015). *Management in Komplexität und Unsicherheit.* Springer: Bad Kreuznach.

WDR (2015). Sport Inside. *WM-Sieg unter Folter* (12.1.2015).

Weiß, O. (1999). Soziale Anerkennung im Sport. In O. Weiß, G. Norden (Hrsg.), *Einführung in die Sportsoziologie* (S. 141-153). WUV: Wien.

Wenzel, O., & Kitsch, Ch. (2011). https://www.bild.de/sport/fussball/schalke/rangnick-sagte-in-der-kabine-ich-habe-keine-kraft-mehr-20097938.bild.html (22.09.2011), Einsicht am: 25.3.2022.

Williams, V. (2020). https://hobbeasy.de/tennis-zitate-und-sprueche/ (13.7.2020), Einsicht am: 20.2.2022.

Windmann, A. (2018). „Die Sache mit dem Brechreiz, es ist das erste Mal, dass ich darüber spreche". *Spiegel, 11.* https://www.spiegel.de/sport/per-mertesacker-von-arsenal-london-ueber-die-haerten-des-fussbal-lerlebens-a-00000000-0002-0001-0000-000156211278, Einsicht am: 14.1.2022.

Wippert, P.-M. (2008). Biographische Brüche und Sport. In K.Weis, R. Gugutzer (Hrsg.), *Handbuch Sportsoziologie* (S. 249-256). Hofmann: Schorndorf.

Wippert, P.-M. (2002). *Karriereverlust und Krise.* Hofmann: Schorndorf.

World Health Organization (2019). *Burn-out an „occupational phenomenon": International Classification of Diseases.* https://www.who.int/news/item/28-05-2019-burn-out-an-occupational-phenomenon-international-classification-of-diseases (28.5.2019), Einsicht am: 28.3.2022.

Yerkes, R. M., & Dodson, J. D. (1908). The relation of strength of stimulus to rapidity of habit-formation. *Journal of Comparative Neurology and Psychology, 18,* 459-482.

ZDF Sportstudio Reportage, (30.1.2022), 17.10-18.00 Uhr.

INDEX

A

Activation	21, 23, 29, 30f., 57, 71
Agitation	34
Anger	44, 94, 117, 145, 152f., 156f.
Anticipation	37, 118
Anxiety	46, 71, 173
Atmosphere	31, 46, 51, 71, 78, 88, 91, 205
Autogenic training	46, 71
Autonomy	84, 109, 126, 243, 252

B

Body language	131, 158 et seq., 183
Breathing relaxation	25 et seq.
Burnout	29, 150, 234 et seq., 250

C

Career	13 et seq., 32, 37, 42, 77, 81, 92, 144, 149, 158, 180f., **208 et seq.**, 217f., 222f., 231, **240 et seq.**, **246 et seq.**, 252
Choking under pressure	148
Commitment	86, 199
Confidence	38, 48, 51, 121, 189, 205, **226 et seq.**
Conviction of self-efficacy	126, 172
Coping	237, 238, 250

D

Deutsche Sporthilfe	49, 242
Disappointment	81, 91, 115f., 152, 177

E

Embodiment	160
Emotion	117, 130, 152, 156, 160 et seq., 183, 238

F

Fans	34, 51, 56, 62, 75, 79, 143, 145, 148, 151, 170, 191, 209, 220
Fear	34 et seq., 58, 71, 130, 135, 150, 161, 193, 216, 231, 236
Flow	25, 33, 51, 75, **123 et seq.**, 126, 127, 203, 214
Focus	25, 27, 41, 64, 66, 107 et seq., 127, 165f., 170, 183, 203, 228
Form of the day	13, 49, 69, 71, 93, 126, 140, 142, 182, 208, 212
Frustration	49, 64, 117, 152 et seq., 160 et seq., 243

G

German Athletes' Support	49, 242
Goals	11, 29, 33, 74, 84 et seq., 88f., 94, 97, **101 et seq.**, 126, 190, 199, 211, 233

H

Habituation	51

I

Immunization training	150
Individual zones of optimal functioning	21
Injury	85, 109, 151, 217, **223 et seq.**, 243, 252

L

Loss aversion	148
Loss of form	237
Luck	12, 74, 117, 122f., 125, 127, 211, 214f.

M

Mindfulness (techniques) 46, 71, 173
Monotony 112 et seq., 127
Motivated by failure 178,
Motivation 14, 34, 85f., **88 et seq.**, **97 et seq.**, 109, 118, 126, 225, 232f., 240
Music 32f., 56, 71, 87, 170, 203, 237

O

Optimal fit 178, 183
Overtraining 234

P

Panic attack 38
Perspective 13, 41, 61, 71, 120, 174, 179, 213, 224, 238, 250
Prediction training 190
Pressure 10, 40, 46, 66, 68, 79 et seq., 88, 106, **143 et seq.**, 178, 182, 186 et seq., 205, 209, 233 et seq., 254
Pre-start condition 22, 71
Progressive muscle relaxation 24 et seq., 71
Psyching up 30, 71

Q

Qualify 42, 71f., 173

R

Reframing 58, 71, 72
Relaxation 25f., 36, 45f., 50, 71, 131, 238
Resilience 36, 134f., 160, 182
Responsibility 15, 187f.
Ritual **192 et seq.**, 197, 205
Routine 22, 28, **192 et seq.**, 197, 205
Ruminate 178

S

Salutogenesis 36
Self-confidence 53, 65, 135, 160, 177, 182, 189, 198
Self-efficacy 85, 107, 189
Shyness 34
Singularity 42, 148, 155, 182, 186 et seq., 205
Singularity training 148, 187, 191
Somatic marker 177
State anxiety 38
Success 11 et seq., 48, 70, 86, 95, 97f., 112, 114, 116 et seq., **177 et seq.**, **208 et seq.**, **214 et seq.**, 237, 249, 252
Success-motivated 180

T

Talent 11, 86, **95 et seq.**, 115, 126, 178, 240
Tension 28, 34, 37, **40 et seq.**, 71, 144, 146
Ten thousand hours 112
Trait anxiety 38
Transactional stress model 238

V

Vision 84, 86f., 100, 126
Visualization 161, 164, 198, 202, 216, 225, **252**
Volition 87, 94, 235

W

Willpower 12, 72, 87, 94, 134

Z

Zen Buddhism 114, 142

CREDITS

Cover and interior design:	Anja Elsen
Layout:	DiTech Publishing Services, www.ditechpubs.com
Cover image:	picture alliance / dpa | Marijan Murat
Managing editor:	Elizabeth Evans
Copy editor:	Sarah Tomblin, www.sarahtomblinediting.com
Translator:	AAA Translation, www.aaatranslation.com

MORE TOP BOOKS ON

ISBN 978-1-78255-248-2
$34.95 US

ISBN 978-1-78255-263-5
$16.95 US

ISBN 978-1-78255-228-4
$21.95 US

ISBN 978-1-78255-108-9
$35.00 US

All information subject to change. © Adobe Stock

MEYER & MEYER SPORT

MEYER & MEYER Sport
Von-Coels-Str. 390
52080 Aachen
Germany

Phone	+49 02 41 - 9 58 10 - 13
Fax	+49 02 41 - 9 58 10 - 10
E-Mail	sales@m-m-sports.com
Website	www.m-m-sports.com

COACHING AND PEAK PERFORMANCE

ISBN 978-1-78255-262-8
$28.95 US

ISBN 978-1-78255-259-8
$19.95 US

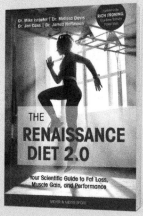

ISBN 978-1-78255-190-4
$26.95 US

ISBN 978-1-78255-257-4
$18.95 US

MEYER & MEYER Sport
Von-Coels-Str. 390
52080 Aachen
Germany

Phone   +49 02 41 - 9 58 10 - 13
Fax   +49 02 41 - 9 58 10 - 10
E-Mail   sales@m-m-sports.com
Website   www.m-m-sports.com

MEYER
& MEYER
SPORT

COGNITIVE TRAINING, CREATIVITY, AND GAME INTELLIGENCE IN SPORTS

All information subject to change. © Adobe Stock

ISBN 978-1-78255-221-5
$19.95 US

ISBN 978-1-78255-258-1
$19.95 US

ISBN 978-1-78255-264-2
$24.95 USS

Coming 2025!

MEYER & MEYER SPORT

MEYER & MEYER Sport
Von-Coels-Str. 390
52080 Aachen
Germany

Phone	+49 02 41 - 9 58 10 - 13
Fax	+49 02 41 - 9 58 10 - 10
E-Mail	sales@m-m-sports.com
Website	www.m-m-sports.com

BEST IN SPORT NARRATIVES

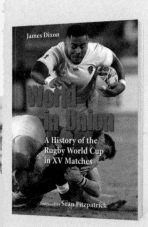

ISBN 978-1-78255-265-9
$24.95 US

ISBN 978-1-78255-227-7
$19.95 US

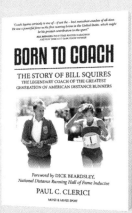

ISBN 978-1-78255-196-6
$28.95 US

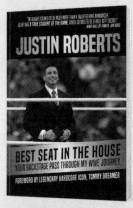

ISBN 978-1-78255-115-7
$24.95 US

MEYER & MEYER Sport
Von-Coels-Str. 390
52080 Aachen
Germany

Phone   +49 02 41 - 9 58 10 - 13
Fax   +49 02 41 - 9 58 10 - 10
E-Mail   sales@m-m-sports.com
Website   www.m-m-sports.com

MEYER
& MEYER
SPORT